The Visitor's Guide
to
Spain:
MALLORCA, MENORCA, IBIZA and FORMENTERA

VISITOR'S GUIDE

SPAIN:
MALLORCA, MENORCA,
IBIZA and FORMENTERA

ANDY GERALD GRAVETTE

MPC
HUNTER
PUBLISHING INC

Published by:
Moorland Publishing Co Ltd,
Moor Farm Road West,
Ashbourne,
Derbyshire DE6 1HD
England

ISBN 0 86190 446 X (paperback)

Colour origination by:
P. & W. Graphics Ltd, Singapore

Printed in the UK by:
Butler & Tanner Ltd,
Frome, Somerset

Published in the USA by:
Hunter Publishing Inc,
300 Raritan Centre Parkway,
CN 94, Edison, NJ 08818
ISBN 1 55650 471 3 (USA)

British Library Cataloguing in
Publication Data:
Gravette, Andy
  The visitor's guide to Spain:
  Mallorca, Menorca, Ibiza and
  Formentera. — (Visitor's Guides)
  I. Title II. Series
  946.04

Cover photograph:
Mirador d'es Colomer, Mallorca
(International Photobank).

Illustrations on pp 11, 15, 18, 19, 34,
35, 39 (lower), 43 (upper), 54
(lower), 55, 58, 59, 62, 63, 66, 67, 71,
79 (lower), 86 (lower) are from the
MPC Picture Collection. All other
illustrations supplied by the
author, Yvonne Gravette, Jolanda
Davies and the Spanish Tourist
Board.

Acknowledgments

The author wishes to thank
Inmaculada Felip and Luisa
Fernandez of the Spanish Tourist
Board in London, Linda De
Saegher of IBATUR and Anna
Skidmore of the Formento del
Turismo de Mallorca for their kind
assistance in providing informa-
tion. Acknowledgments are also
due to IBERIA Airlines of Spain
and 3M Scotch Film.

CONTENTS

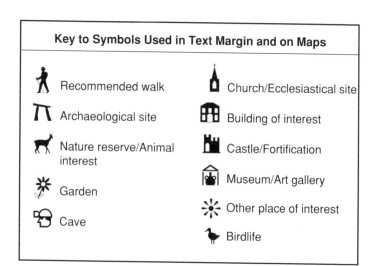

Key to Symbols Used in Text Margin and on Maps

Recommended walk

Archaeological site

Nature reserve/Animal interest

Garden

Cave

Church/Ecclesiastical site

Building of interest

Castle/Fortification

Museum/Art gallery

Other place of interest

Birdlife

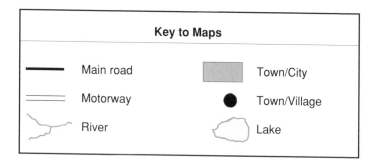

Key to Maps

Main road

Motorway

River

Town/City

Town/Village

Lake

Note on the maps

The maps drawn for each chapter, while comprehensive, are not designed to be used as route maps, but rather to locate the main towns, villages and places of interest.

1

SPAIN'S BALEARIC ISLANDS

Holiday brochures herald the message of hedonistic holidays and inexpensive package deals to a little group of islands within easy reach of most of western Europe. Tucked into a corner of the Mediterranean under the shadow of the Iberian peninsula, the Balearic Islands are dwarfed in size by other popular resort islands such as Corsica, Sardinia, Sicily, Crete or Cyprus, yet over the past few years the tourist trade of these islands has outstripped those of many other places in Europe. Tourism to the Balearic Islands even outstrips that to more exotic destinations like the Caribbean or the Indian Ocean islands.

What is the attraction of these tiny Spanish outposts? Is it the brashness of Mallorca's nightlife and entertainments; Menorca's secluded coves and curious megaliths; the trendy boutiques, restaurants and clubs of Ibiza; or Formentera's rocky landscapes and wide expanses of white sandy beach. Apart from Formentera, the three other islands offer the visitor a choice of the high life, deserted bays, prehistoric monuments, shops, department stores, bistros, nightclubs, wild country walks, stunning beaches, secret caves and a wealth of historic sites.

In addition to these attractions each island has a separate identity lodged in its traditions, its unique architecture and the island people who have established themselves as friendly and easy going with tourists, wise and knowledgeable with the historian and wildlife enthusiast, and skilled and hardy in the arts, crafts and traditional occupations which formed their particular culture and lifestyle. The discerning traveller with the help of this book can benefit from the rich selection of sights, sounds, tastes and feeling that each island and its people can offer.

Midway between the Catalan coast of eastern Spain and the Algerian coast of North Africa, four main islands of Mallorca, Menorca, Ibiza and Formentera, together with their satellite islets make up the Balearic archipelago. In total land area the islands are a little smaller than their sisters in the Atlantic, the Canary Islands, with 5,014sq km (1,936sq miles) between them.

Located in the western arm of the Mediterranean Sea, these islands have lent their name to the waters in which they sit — the Balearic Sea. The islands form a string across this part of the Mediterranean for about 320km (200 miles). Menorca, the second largest island and the most northerly, is separated from Mallorca by 34km (21 miles) of sea. Mallorca is the largest island and lies 85km (53 miles) north-east of the third largest isle, Ibiza. In turn, Ibiza's tiny sister island, Formentera, is just 4km (2½ miles) to the south. Cabrera, a tiny islet, is just 18km (11 miles) off Mallorca's southern coast.

The popularity of the islands is due in the main to their coastline — 1,240 kilometres (770 miles) of sandy beaches, rocky coves and spectacular cliffs. The proximity of the islands to the mainland also means that access from most European capitals is no more than a few hour's flight. Barcelona, just 248km (154 miles) to the north of Palma de Mallorca, is the nearest large city and there are regular flights from every European capital.

Each island has its individual geological character and each possesses its own particular variety of landscape which offers the visitor a choice of mountain scenery, flat agricultural plateaux, sweeping fine-sanded beaches, secluded bays, sheltered coves and wild craggy coastlines. The topography, Mediterranean climate and wildlife of these islands not only attracts fun-seekers and wealthy yachtsmen, but also lures lovers of history, sports enthusiasts, discerning gourmets, those seeking peace and quite, and students of natural history.

Fauna and Flora

It is almost impossible to ignore the natural history of the islands. Even in the narrow lanes of the towns, there are colourful singing birds in little cages hung outside verandas, or balanced on window sills high above the bustling streets. The other sound which reminds the traveller of the Mediterranean location is the chirping of the cicadas on balmy evenings. Draped over aged walls, pink, white and purple oleander and bougainvillea cascade in great splashes of colour, while deep green cypress, juniper and fig trees seem to sprout from the very foundations of ancient whitewashed churches. In city courtyards and town plazas gnarled olive trees provide shade while date palms line many a boulevard or *avenida*.

The variety of natural produce in the markets is testament to the fact that, although tourism has brought the brashness of the modern world, the islanders are traditionally bound to the land and sea. Yellow mimosa, pink and white almond blossom, peach cyclamen, orange daisies, crimson hibiscus, electric-blue morning glory, gold sunflowers and gladioli in impossible shades cram the stalls, and this is but a selection of the flowers which grow wild in this temperate climate. Cultivated plants include brilliant geraniums, petunias, blue irises, honeysuckle and multi-coloured dahlias. Particular features of the Balearic landscape include the cactus-like prickly pear, the gaunt carob trees, mastic trees, ilex, myrtle and the ever-present pines.

Swordfish, tunny, squid, octopus, langoustine, grouper and red mullet may be unfamiliar fare to the visitor from colder climes, yet here the dockside stalls groan under catches of exotic fish from the warm Balearic Sea. Scuba divers and snorkellers can appreciate the colours of these and smaller fish and marine life in the wild because of the clarity of the waters off most of the shores. Vegetables and fruit stalls include fresh grapes, local oranges and lemons, olives, prickly pears, figs, almonds, melons, peppers and tomatoes.

However, it is out in the islands' countryside that the visitor begins to appreciate the vast variety of flora and wildlife which is either indigenous or is attracted to these temperate lands. It is not by chance that the Balearic Islands have become one of Europe's leading orthinological centres. The Grup Balear d'Ornitologia i Defensa de la Naturalesa (GOB) promote the protection and conservation of the islands' natural history, as well as encouraging visiting ornithologists. Large numbers of visiting birdwatchers come to observe the many migrant species from waders such as curlew, sandpiper and plover, to more exotic birds like the Egyptian vulture, honey buzzard, hobby, marsh harrier or the flamingo. Familiar sightings in the countryside include the colourful bee eater, hoopoes, finches, doves and pigeons. Much more difficult to spot are the islands' famous booted eagles, peregrine falcons, red kites and ospreys. The coastal regions provide ideal habitats for all manner of wildfowl and seabird, including ducks, geese, egrets, herons and the scarce Audouin's gull.

Wild mammals are rather scarce on these islands apart from

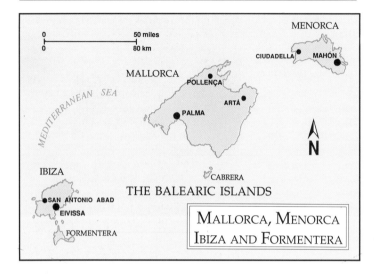

familiar species such as bats, mice, rabbit, hare and hedgehog. A prehistoric breed of antelope once roamed here but today the largest non-domestic animals to be seen are the seals which haunt the coves and caves of the rocky coasts or the friendly dolphin, often seen following the wake of sailing boats. Less easily seen are the Mediterranean sea turtle, whose numbers are rapidly diminishing. On land the hiker might be lucky enough to see a rare native tortoise on Menorca, or one of the island's four breeds of snake. More common throughout the islands are various species of Balearic lizard, and geckos which dart across walls and ceilings in search of some of the prolific insects life which thrives in this moderate climate.

History

A prehistoric cattle-like creature was the first large animal to adapt to the conditions of these small islands off the coast of mainland Spain. For a thousand years or so years until their extinction, they co-existed with a Neolithic species of man which inhabited the Balearic Islands around 5000BC. Six thousand years ago a pre-ceramic civilization developed in the Islands and two thousand years later, around 2000BC, a ceramic culture flourished on the main islands. This coincided with the advent of metal working skills and led to what is known as the Copper Age.

The exact date of the arrival of the famous Talayot society re-

Locally grown oranges, lemons and other produce are sold at the many markets on the islands

Cacti, suculents and other tender plants grow profusely in the warm climate

PREHISTORIC SITES ON THE BALEARIC ISLANDS

An important aspect of the Balearic Islands which is largely unknown to the visitors who throng the resorts and beaches are the unique archaeological sites.

Talayots

These are tall, tapering tower-like monuments, which may have been used as watchtowers, although their exact purpose is not always clear. Some have a low doorway leading to a small chamber, while others are solid with no chamber or doorway. *Talayots* are often associated with other stone structures and are usually surrounded by a low wall. There are *talayot* sites on Mallorca, but many more on Menorca.

Taulas

A *taula* is a huge T-shaped stone structure made from two massive slabs of rock some $2^1/_2$-4m (9-13ft) high, and often near *talayots*. They are often associated with other stone structures, and were always built on high ground. The stones have been carefully worked and the uprights were set in grooves in the bedrock for stability. They are found on Menorca where seven remain in their original position out of an original thirty or so.

Navetas

These are prehistoric tombs with a low entrance and two inner chambers, one above the other. *Navetas* are so named because they resemble upturned boats, and they were mostly built in isolated areas. About ten remain in good condition on Menorca, and a few exist on Mallorca.

Dolmen, Sepulchres and Dwellings

On Mallorca, Menorca, Ibiza and Formentera there are vestiges of prehistoric occupation represented by dwellings such as the village remains at Capocorp Vell near Llucmajor on Mallorca, a similar site on Ibiza in San José called the Punta Jondal, and the remains of circular prehistoric houses on Formentera. On Formentera there is a Megalithic sepulchre, while on Ibiza there is an ancient dolmen, Can Pelleu, at San Jorge.

sponsible for the numerous remarkable megaliths and stone structures found predominantly on Menorca and Mallorca, is a matter of debate but some of the remains of that culture certainly date to around 1500BC. These people formed the nucleus of a Bronze Age culture which coincided with the appearance of another society known as the Beaker Culture. These people developed a remarkable dexterity with the slingshot and became known throughout the Mediterranean, and particularly with the visiting Phoenecians, for their ability to defend themselves with this weapon.

Later the Romans also admired their skill with the sling and, in 406BC, the Cartheginian General Hannibal recruited 5,000 Balearic slingsmen to aid him in his campaigns against Sicily. The Talayots were initially a Bronze Age culture but developed through a thousand years into an Iron Age society which was to last until the coming of the Romans in the early part of the first century BC. The Greeks, also familiar with the islander's ability with the sling, dubbed the islands ' The Balearics' from the Greek word *ballein* — to sling.

It is related in Diodorus Siculus' *Universal History*, written around 65BC, that the slingsmen of these islands were armed with three slings, one in the hand, one around the waist and another tied around the head. The sling, however accurate and however deadly, was eventually no match for the legionaires of Quintus Cecilius Metullus who conquered the Balearics Islands in 123BC.

The invasion of Vandals from the Baltic regions followed Roman occupation and two major raids were made by them on the islands in 425 and 426AD. Belisarius, a Byzantine general under the Emperor Justinian, wrested the Balearic Islands from the German Vandals and they became part of the Byzantium Empire in 534AD. For two hundred years the islands remained protected by Byzantium until, with increasing pressure from Moorish raiders, from around 708 until 902AD, the Eastern Roman Empire relinquished its hold.

The Balearic Islands fell to the Arabs in 902AD and the Saracens, under the Caliphate of Cordova, established themselves in the major islands. The islands were declared an Emirate of Moorish Spain in 1075AD.

In September 1229 King Jaime I, ' El Conquistador', led an official crusade to the islands after several skirmishes with Moorish galleys off the Spanish coast. Five hundred Catalan ships sailed to Palma de Mallorca and, by 31 December 1229, Mallorca was finally taken. The other islands finally capitulated and Ibiza was captured in 1235 by Guillem de Montgri. In 1287 King Alphonso III conquered the island of Menorca and King Jaime II ruled the islands until his death in 1311.

Ramon Llull, the island's most famous son, mystic and missionary was martyred in 1315 on the Barbary coast. The Catalan King Sanchez ruled for 13 years until 1324. King Jaime III, who ruled from 1324, was killed in 1349 while quelling an uprising on Mallorca and he was the last real king of the Balearic islands.

During the middle ages the islands went into a steep decline and they were left in a backwater to endure the hardships of loss of trade, the ravages of the Black Death, and a civil war from 1450 until 1453. The Spanish Inquisition was to follow in 1484, which continued its vengeful deeds until 1517.

Trading interest was focussed elsewhere — Columbus, said by the islanders to have been born on Mallorca: in Genova, or Porto Colom, or sometimes in Soller, discovered the New World of the Americas in 1492, and riots erupted on Mallorca in 1521. In 1535 the famous pirate Barbarossa sacked Mahon on Menorca and then Ciudadella in 1558. Turkish attacks on Ibiza followed for the next twenty years, but towards the end of the century King Philip II gained absolute control over the Mediterranean Sea and the Balearic Islands.

In 1708 the island of Menorca was taken by the English who held almost unbroken sway on the island for around a century. Mallorca followed the Spanish mainland in surrendering to King Philip V's forces in 1715 after the War of Spanish Succession. A riot rocked Ibiza in 1749 and, in 1756, the French captured Menorca during the Seven Years' War only to return it to England in 1768 when it was exchanged for Cuba and the Philippines. Menorca was returned to Spain in 1802.

It was about a century later that the islands began to attract the first tourists which, today, outnumber the indigenous population more than eight times.

Population, Politics and Economy

The major islands of the Balearics have had many names down through the centuries and today many people are undecided as to their correct spelling. In fact there is no officially correct way as even the Balearic Island Tourist Board use a variety of spellings — Mallorca (Majorca), Menorca (Minorca) and Ibiza (Eivissa). The five main islands and the 150 or so tiny islets which comprise the Islas Baleares are divided as a Spanish Province, into sixty-five municipalities — fifty-two on Mallorca, seven on the island of Menorca, five

Off-the-beaten track hamlets are still to be found on the Balearic islands, such as this roadside church in northern Mallorca

on Ibiza and one on Formentera. The total population of the Balearic Islands is estimated at around 750,000, comprised of 601,000 Mallorquins, 67,000 Menorquins, 77,000 Ibizencos and 5,000 Formenterans. Population density on the 5,000sq km (1,936sq miles) of land is around 150 per square kilometre.

The people of the islands speak a dialect of Catalan Spanish which varies from island to island, but the official language is Castillian Spanish as it is throughout mainland Spain. English is understood throughout the islands and particularly in the areas more frequented by tourists.

Although the age-old industries of fishing, salt production, agriculture, shoemaking, costume jewellery, textiles and ceramic manufacture prevail, tourism has changed and is still changing the face of the islands and with it the inhabitant's reliance on traditional skills and natural products. The people are resigned to the fact that the tourism industry is here to stay and the islands now attract almost a sixth of the number of tourists which visit mainland Spain.

Food and Drink

At a banquet on the Spanish mainland, in 1228, King Jaime I's table was loaded with Balearic Island produce. So impressed was the king with the variety and quality of the food that he immediately resolved to capture the islands for his throne. A year later, with 500 ships, Jaime took Mallorca and, from then on, the king, no doubt, was liberally supplied with all the delicacies the islanders could produce! Testament to this is recorded in the name of Palma's second largest castle, Castillo Bendinat, a corruption of *Be Hem Dinat* — 'We have eaten well' — which was King Jaime I's comment after his first meal on Mallorca in the banqueting room of this ancient castle.

The 'Isles of the Spice of Life' could not be a better accolade for these fertile lands which have given the world *salsa mahonesa* — mayonaise, a name derived from its city of origin, Mahon, on Menorca — and garum, that most pungent of spicy and aromatic *salsas* or sauces which originated in Ibiza. On all the islands the highly spiced *sobrasada* or minced pork sausage could be called the local fare and most local restaurants offer this, together with a selection from paella, a stew or soup, a rice dish of sorts, a local fish dish and, the classic Balearic speciality, roast sucking pig.

For snacks one can choose the ubiqitous *tapas* or mouthsize appetizers, the *empanada*, or filled pasty, a *flao*, a cheese pastry from Ibiza, Menorca's *galletas*, a type of oily biscuit, or Mallorca's *cocas de patatas*, a potato-bread concoction.

One often has to divert from the beaten tourist track in order to enjoy some of the really traditional island culinary delights such as *ensaimada*, a spiral-shaped, sugared, flaky pastry bread which comes in a variety of sizes; *tumbet*, a stew with aubergines, peppers, potatoes and pumkin; *trempo*, a mixed salad of tomatoes, onions, apples, pears, peppers and purslane; *greizonera de peix*, a popular fish stew, or *greizonera de frare*, a meat and vegetable stew. In some coastal areas *greizonera d'anguila*, eel stew, is a favourite dish, while inland *greizonera de peius de porc*, pigs trotters, cheese and breadcrumb stew may be a typical meal. However, because of the demands of tourists, many local dishes have almost been replaced by the ubiquitous fast food. The Balearics can also be called the 'Islands of Salt', a precious commodity which they have supplied to the world since before Roman times. The great variety of cured pork sausages, local ham and preserves show that the islands still utilise some of the 60,000 tons per year produced at Las Salinas on Ibiza.

While the sun evaporates the sea water to produce salt, it also ripens cereals, vegetables and fruits, especially oranges and lemons, as well as grapes from which the local wines are made. However, only Mallorca produces wine in any commercial quantity and, although local vineyards produce a selection of wines, the most commonly drunk wine is the Rioja from the north of Spain. *Sangria*, made from wine, brandy, orange and lemon juice is an appetizing drink, while liqueurs like *hierba* — made from herbs, and *palo* — made from carobs, are both popular accompaniments to the local dark coffee.

Sport, Leisure and Entertainment

In the distant past the Balearic Islanders developed one particular sport which made them famous throughout the ancient world. This was the art of the slingshot. Legend has it that the islands' youths were taught the skill of the sling by their parents placing their food high in the branches of trees. If the young boys were accurate shots then they would be able to dislodge their meals and so have sufficient to eat — the poorer *hondero* or stone throwers starved.

Not lost or forgotten, the skill of the slingshot, *tiro con honda*, is still practiced in the islands. There are special courses given in the art and slingshot competitions are held regularly in Palma de Mallorca.

Today the authorities appreciate that not all visitors come only for the sun, sand and sea; and also that the people who live on the island wish to enjoy the local entertainment, cultural displays and sporting activities. On the largest island, in Mallorca's capital, Palma, the

Away from the tourist ⇒ areas life still follows its traditional pattern. Off to Sunday Mass in Artá, Mallorca

Carriage rides are popular with tourists

The Balearic Islands have a great diversity of landscape; here are the rugged limestone mountains of Mallorca's Sierra de San Vicente

PLACE NAMES ON THE BALEARIC ISLANDS

Visitors to the Balearic Islands will come across many of the following words, especially on road signs. The official language is Castillian Spanish, but on the islands Catalan is widely used. Road signs may be in official Spanish, but often overpainted with the Catalan version. Place names on maps and other literature are highly inconsistent, often depending on whether they are produced nationally or locally. In particular places named after a saint can be written as Santo (male), Santa (female), San, Sto, Sta or S.

English	Spanish (Castilian)	Local Catalan
Airport	Aeropuerto	Aeroport
Bay (small)	Cala	
Bay	Bahia	
Beach	Playa	Platja
Bridge	Puente	Pont
Cape	Cabo	Cap de
Castle	Castillo	
Cave	Cueva	Cova
Church	Iglesia	Esglèsia
Coast	Costa	
Estate of		Son
Farm	Finca	
Harbour	Puerto	Port
Hermitage	Ermita	
House of	Casa	Ca'n (Casa d'en)
Mountain peak	Pico	Puig
Mountain range	Sierra	Serra
Market	Mercado	
Museum	Museo	
Path	Vía	Via
River	Río	Riu
Road	Camino	Cami
Square	Plaza	Plasa
Stream	Torrente	
Street	Calle	Carrer
Town	Cuidad	Pueblo
Town Hall	Ayuntamiento	Ajuntament
Viewpoint	Mirador	
Watchtower	Atalayas	Talaias/Talayot

selection of sport, leisure, entertainment and cultural events is equal to that of many cities twice its size. From traditional bull fights and inevitable football matches, to ballet, opera and folklore performance, from pop-rock concerts and theatrical events to greyhound racing and golf tournaments, Palma provides for every diversion. Tennis matches are held in its spacious tennis club and the city's three main sailing clubs hold regular regattas. Palma's nightlife includes more than ten cinemas, restaurants of a dozen or more nationalities, assorted bars, pubs and discos, and a selection of casinos, nightclubs, cabarets and spectaculars ranging from local flamenco displays to those of a more intimate nature!

Not every island has such a variety of entertainment and leisure but the selection in most main towns is more than enough for most visitors. For example, Ibiza only has one golf course while there are four on Menorca, whereas Ibiza has three horse riding schools but Menorca has only one.

For the sports-minded, the Balearic Islands hold national competitions in just about everything from hunting and cycling, to horse riding and motorcycling. The Balearic Office of Tourism produces a comprehensive list of all sporting federations with contacts and telephone numbers.

Pelota, locally known as *Basque Ball*, *petanca*, or *petanque*, and *tiro con honda* (slingshot), are the national sports of the Balearic Islands but, because of their international status, and the demand of tourists and visitors, the islanders have adopted every sort of sporting activity as a national pastime. Most of the larger hotels offer their own facilities like football or basketball fields, tennis courts, golf courses and water sports activities. Many hotels also provide a range of entertainment from traditional folk dancing to musical spectaculars and pop music concerts.

Facilities for tourists include almost forty tennis clubs, and a similar number of sailing clubs. The Balearic Islands can also boast sixty marinas with well over 12,000 berths and there will soon be a total of fifteen golf courses on Mallorca, Menorca and Ibiza.

For indoor activities the islanders hold chess, billiards, bridge and darts tournaments. Squash is a favourite with the more active and many hotels have squash courts as well as table tennis facilities, although they are more often played outdoors. As for entertainment, the Balearics Council of Culture, Education and Sports produces a colourful, helpful and inexpensive guide to what's on throughout the islands.

Folkloric entertainment is a favourite with visitors as the local costumes are colourful and the performances energetic and melodious. Traditional dress for the men consists of a black waistcoat over a voluminous shirt worn with a bright cumberbund and striped, baggy pantaloons, topped by a black, wide-brimmed hat. On some islands the mode changes to a bright red pom-pommed cloth cap and plain white pants. A gaily embroidered shawl and headscarf is worn by the women. Variations on the headscarf include a lace item of clothing which doubles as a collar, and country women often adopt a wide-brimmed straw hat worn over the headscarf. The skirt and blouse are conventionally of a dark material, often locally dyed, and a striped apron usually completes the costume.

The local Balearic music is distinctive and haunting. Traditionally a dance group or band will include the inevitable guitar, or lute-like mandolin. The large, engraved castanets accompanying most groups are known as *castanyoles* and the local version of the drum is called the *espasi*. A *cantador* sings, with the backing of the *sonador*, a player who demonstrates his skill on the *xeremia*, a type of flute, and the *espasi* at the same time.

One peculiar local instrument, often played unaccompanied, is *el chirimillero*, a form of bagpipes called, simply, a 'goatsack'. Traditional dances include the *curta* and the *larga* but the more universally famous Spanish dance is the flamenco.

2

MALLORCA

M allorca (or Majorca), is the largest of the Balearic Islands and has a population of 610,000 on its 3,639sq km (1,405sq miles). With 500km (310 miles) of coastline constituting the island's major attraction, combined with its climate which ranges between 10°C (50°F) and 60°C (79°F), Mallorca hosts many thousands of visitors throughout the year. The good-natured Mallorquins and their easy going attitude to foreigners and tourists have contributed to the popularity of this island.

Mallorca offers a wide variety of landscapes, from the rugged mountains of the Sierra de San Vicente in the Tramontana region of the north-west, to the rolling hills of the Sierra de Levante in the east. The wide open spaces of Mallorca's central plain make travelling across the island easy and tourists flock to the resort areas of the Pollença region on the north coast, to the bays and sandy beaches along Mallorca's east coast, and to the cliffs and secluded coves forming the island's western shores. Spectacular limestone caves are to be found in the east; in the north and west coloured cliffs and sea arches decorate the coast; in the far south the salt flats of the Salinas de Levante and hot springs of the Balneario de Sant Joan de la Font Santa provide spectacular contrasts.

Of all the Balearic Islands, Mallorca attracts most ornithologists for its diversity of both indigenous and migratory birdlife which have chosen the island for its convenient geographical location and variety of habitats. Fishing and sailing are popular pastimes and there are now twenty-three established harbours, while the sea teems with a bewildering number of species of fish.

Around the coast there are several tiny islets. Off the south-west tip of the island is the miniscule Isla Dragonera and off the southern coast is the Cabrera Archipelago. Comprising seventeen islets, Cabrera itself is the largest. The other main islet in this group is Conjera — 'Rabbit's Warren' — and this lies between Cabrera and the Mallorcan coast. A sea cave on Cabrera is famed for its curious illuminations which once attracted tourists as a beauty spot. Today, however, Cabrera is a military outpost and visitors are forbidden, apart from scientific expeditions, to visit the archipelago.

Mallorca's capital, Palma de Mallorca is called the *Ciutat* by islanders as it is the capital of the entire Balearic Islands. Located at the head of the Bahia de Palma, a large semi-circular bay which attracts a good proportion of the island's tourists, Palma has a fine, wide harbour, a marina and an international airport close by.

History

It was on Mallorca that a curious civilization known as the Talayots established themselves. This prehistoric culture specialised in constructing towns with extensive ramparts and *talayots*, or fortified towers. This civilisation dates from around 1400BC and evidence of this culture can be seen at several sites around the island, which include a few examples of *navetas* or burial mounds.

The Bronze Age was followed by the Iron Age and during this period the tribes developed their skill with the slingshot. The Carthe-ginians and Romans came later, and in 123BC Quintus Cecilius Metellus landed on Mallorca (named by the Romans Majorca or 'Major' compared with the smaller Minorca or 'Minor').

A succession of invaders occupied the island over the next thousand years from the Vandals of northern Europe, and Visigoths from the north-east to the Moors, who had settled in the Spanish peninsula. Al Khaulani, the Moorish leader under the Emirate of Cordova, eventually took Mallorca in the name of Islam in 902AD and a trading post was established on the island during the 300 years of Moorish domination. The Christians, under the auspices of King Jaime I of Aragon, succeeded the Moors in 1229 and a government was installed on Mallorca.

Mallorca soon developed into a strong political and trading centre, acquiring the status of a kingdom, and its influence extended over parts of Spain and France. Mallorcan trading links expanded during medieval times and the city of Palma (then known as *Ciutat*) became a focal point for western Mediterranean merchantmen. Short-lived wealth was followed by a series of setbacks. In 1343 King Jaime III was ousted from the Kingdom of Mallorca by Pedro IV of Aragon. Tragically, the Black Death decimated a large proportion of the population in the mid-fourteenth century.

From 1450 until 1453 civil war held Mallorca in its grip, while thirty years later the Spanish Inquisition introduced more violence to the island, and in 1521 riots spread through Mallorca. For many years the island suffered a crippling economic and social decline. Mallorca was fortified against pirates and attacks by coastal raiders in 1575 and, one hundred years later, a great famine swept through the Western Mediterranean. During the War of Spanish Succession the island of Mallorca traditionally sided with King Charles III of Aragon against the Bourbon King Philip V. In 1715, after Philip had defeated Charles on mainland Spain, Mallorca surrendered.

Under Bourbon rule the island recovered its status as a trading centre. Internal squabbles on the island disrupted its stability during the third quarter of the eighteenth century. A resistance movement emerged and 5,000 French captives, imprisoned on the Isle of Cabrera just off the coast of Mallorca, perished from starvation in 1809.

During the war against Napoleon the Balearic Islands, particularly Mallorca, became a refuge for those fleeing the hostilities. In 1875 the monarchy was restored in mainland Spain and the island settled down to a comparatively stable existence. Just after World War I the first tourists began to take notice of this tranquil island and, apart from the setbacks of the Spanish Civil War and World War II, the Mallorcans have never looked back — apart from being reminded of their past wherever they turn as they are surrounded by numerous historical monuments and early architectural gems.

Accommodation in Mallorca's Resorts

Outside Palma there is no shortage of accommodation. These range from the five-star hotels like the Formentor, in the northern region of the same name and the Melia de Mar, in Illetas, to single-star hostels, private apartments and villas for rent or lease. Both sides of the half moon-shaped Bay of Palma on which the city stands have numerous fine beaches which have attracted more than 300 hotel and residential developments. It is on this particular bay that the majority of the island's visitor accommodation is situated. Including the many hotels and hostels in Palma itself, the deep, wide bay blessed with many beaches and inlets, provides the visitor with a choice of almost 500 holiday and residential establishments.

A short distance south-east of Palma is the town of El Arenal, now

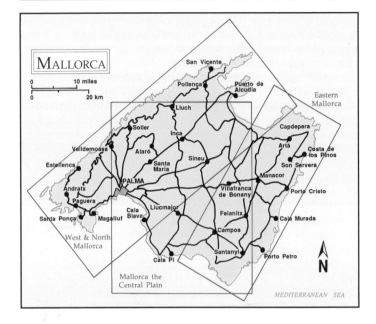

a conglomerate of more than seventy hotels and more than eighty hostels and apartment complexes. The string of resorts on this part of the coast include Las Maravillas with five three-star hotels, Cala Estancia and Cala Gamba which are now almost linked by residential developments. Cala Gamba has just one small hotel. These developments range along the Playas de Mallorca on the east side of the Bay of Palma and almost link to El Arenal in the south through the fifty or so developments of Ca'n Pastilla, stretching along the coastline just a short distance from the airport. On the west side of the bay is the resort area of Playa Magalluf. Here, again the region's twenty apartment blocks and hotels spread along the coast on the attractive bay-strewn promentory. The next development, on its own bay, is the popular Palma Nova. Here there are over forty hotels, hostels and apartment blocks. On the same side of the bay, but closer to Palma, is another resort, Portals Nous, which provides accommodation in ten complexes overlooking the bay. Also with ten hotels and apartment blocks ranging from a five-star hotel to a two-star hostel, is Ses Illetas, a salubrious location because of its position on a promentory. Around the next bay, towards Pelma, is Ca's Catala, with just one four-star hotel and a small hostel. Next door to Ca's

Catala is the resort region of Cala Major, another group of twenty-four hotels, hostels and apartment blocks. Cala Major is within walking distance of the city and offers the full range of accommodation in hotels, hostels and apartments.

The rest of Mallorca can be divided into the coastal regions where the majority of the resort accommodation is located and the five main towns located across the interior of the island. These towns include Sineu, roughly in the centre of Mallorca, and Artá in the east. Also in the east of the island is the town of Felanitx, with three three-star hotels, including the Cala Ferrera, and one single-star hotel. Between Felanitx and Palma is the town of Llucmajor which has accommodation at the three-star Maioris Palm Sol, and the two-star Es Pas.

A short distance west of Palma is the village of Paguera located on the Playa Paguera. This has been developed into a most popular resort which sports a range of accommodation from two four-star hotels, the Gran Hotel Sunna Park and Villamil, to more than a dozen one-star hotels, in all totalling seventy establishments. Between Paguera and Palma Nova or Magalluf is a peninsula where Santa Ponça is located. This resort boasts twenty hotels ranging from four-star to one-star and two attractive hostels. To the west of Paguera is Puerto de Andraitx, another small resort with just three hotels and four hostels and residential hostels.

On the straight road north from Palma to the popular northern coast is the town of Inca. In Inca there is just one small hostel but most visitors continue through Inca to the beach resorts of the Bahia de Pollença and the Cabos Formentor and Pinar. To one side of Cabo Pinar is the Bahia de Alcudia on which are located several resorts. The town of Alcúdia has only three small places for accommodation as most visitors stay in the twenty-five hotels and hostels in the harbour village of Puerto de Alcúdia. Just around the bay is the large resort of Ca'n Picafort with almost forty establishments ranging from numerous one-star hotels, apartments and hostels to seven three-star hotels. At the far end of the large bay is the small resort of Colonia de San Pedro with just three hostels.

Back in the town of Puerto Pollença there are thirty establishments, about half of which are hotels and the rest hostels. There are eight three-star hotels in Puerto Pollença and in the town of Pollença itself there is just one residential hotel. The famous five-star Hotel Formentor stands on its own north of Pollença on the cape of the same name. Around the point is another beach resort, San Vicente, on Cala Vicente, offering accommodation in nine hotels and hostels.

Although there is little in the way of hotels on the craggy, straight,

MALLORCA'S BEACH RESORTS

The popular, brash, resorts are in the south, mainly around the Bay of Palma and the south-west peninsula. The east coast mainly has family resorts, while in the north they are generally quieter. There are seventy-four officially listed beaches around Mallorca and the tourist board issue a leflet (HI-14) which details the amenities on each beach.

THE SOUTH AND WEST

El Arenal

Very popular with the young with many bars, cafés, fast-food shops and discos, but very noisy at night. There is a smallish beach at the eastern end which gets very crowded. Aqua City water park just outside El Arenal claims to be the largest in the world. Open-air market on Tuesdays.

Ca'n Pastilla

A long sandy beach on the Arenal side, a harbour at the western end and terraced sunbathing area in the centre. Busy and only four miles from the airport. Bars, restaurants, shops and water sports facilities.

Cala Major

There is a wide range of cafés, shops and nightlife along a busy main road. The crowded beach is in a small bay with soft sand which shelves gently into the sea.

San Agustin

A very small sandy beach amongst rocks, with most of the sunbathing on the rocks themselves.

Illetas

An attractive green resort with a small and crowded sand beach in a picturesque bay, but virtually no nightlife.

Palma Nova

A long, narrow beach with fine golden sand which shelves gradually into the sea. A lively resort with many fast-food bars and shops, popular with young people, but noisy at night. Marineland Oceanarium nearby.

Magalluf

A big, brash 'concrete jungle' resort popular with the young, packed with bars, cafés and discos. The beach is wide, set in a bay and crowded. Just outside Magalluf is Aquapark.

Santa Ponça
Attractive small beach with golden sand, popular with families, but some nightlife. Can be noisy and crowded.

Paguera
A busy main road with shops and bars, but smart and clean. Beach is long, narrow and crowded, with darker sand.

Puerto de Andraitx
A large yacht port in a picturesque bay with very small beaches. Quiet during the day, but some chic nightlife. Excellent seafood restaurants.

Puerto Soller
The beach, with sand and shingle, runs around an enclosed bay, with safe bathing. An attractive family resort with shops, bars and restaurants, but busy with day trippers from Palma.

THE EAST

Playa de Canyamel
Fine unspoilt beach, good restaurant nearby, Sea sport facilities.

Cala Bona
A quiet resort with a pleasant harbour used by local fishermen. Beaches are man-made with jetties and coarse sand. Quickly being swamped by the nearby resort of Cala Millor.

Cala Millor
Attractive beach with golden sand, less crowded to the south, with promenade and gardens. Good nightlife.

Porto Cristo
Pleasant yacht harbour, with plenty of cafés, restaurants and shops. The small sandy beach shelves gently, but gets crowded.

Calas de Mallorca
Purpose-built resort in a bay with golden sand, but beach can get crowded. Little nightlife outside the hotels. The sea off-shore can be very dangerous — **do not ignore warnings**.

Cala Murada
Pleasant unspoilt beach.

Cala d'Or
Smart bars, cafés and boutiques around the yacht harbour. Picturesque up-market whitewashed resort. A few small beaches in attractive bays with gently shelving golden sand.

MALLORCA'S BEACH RESORTS — Continued

THE NORTH

Cala Ratjada
Fine harbour near two pleasant, unspoilt little beaches. Restaurants and five hotels.

Ca'n Picafort
Quiet resort with promenade overlooked by tasteless concrete hotels and with many open-air cafés, at southern end of Mallorca's longest beach. Shallow clear sea with some rock pools.

Puerto de Alcúdia
At northern end of 8-mile long beach, with good sand and safe bathing. Hotels, shops and bars are along a busy main road. Yacht harbour.

Puerto Pollença
In a wide bay surrounded by trees and mountains, regarded as one of the most attractive resorts. White sand beaches and promenade with cafés, bars and shops. Larger beach south of the marina which is not crowded. No brash nightlife. Yacht marina.

Cala San Vicente
Two small beaches with soft sand joined by a concrete pathway. Shallow, safe water. Very quiet and isolated resort with only a couple of shops and bars.

Formentor
Long narrow beach backed by pine trees on rocky peninsula. High-class hotel facilites including mini-golf and tennis.

---

western shores of Mallorca, apart from the fifteen hotels and same number of hostels at Soller, about halfway along the coast, it is the east coastline with its little cape and points interspaced with pretty, sandy bays, which attracts a large part of the island's visitors. From the northern point of that coast, Cabo Freu, running south, the first resort area is Cala Ratjada with around seventy-five accommodation establishments ranging from six three-star hotels to numerous single-star hotels and many hostels. Inland from Cala Ratjada is the village of Capdepera which has six hotels and two hostels. Following the coast south, the next developed area is around the Costa de los Pinos where the Eurotel Golf Punta Rotja, offers four-star accommodation. Further down the coast are the resorts of Cala Bona with

fifteen hotels, hostels and apartment blocks and Cala Millor with almost sixty establishments.

The African Reserve Safari Park is located between Cala Millor and the next resort of S'Illot with eight hotels and hostels. The nearest town is Porto Cristo with twenty-two establishments, most of which are small hotels or hostels. The long stretch of Cala Falco divides Porto Cristo from the next popular resort of Porto Colom and Cala Murada. Together, these developments offer a variety of accommodation in fourteen establishments and, not far south, is the vastly popular region which encompasses Cala d'Or, Playa d'Or, Porto Petro, Cala Figuera and Cala Santany. Together, these resorts on this south-eastern region of Mallorca offer a complete range of accommodation from three four-star hotels to a range of about seventy other hotels, hostels and apartments.

Around the point called the Cabo de Salinas, heading west towards Palma, is the resort area of Colonia de Sant Jordi with fifteen establishments from three-star hotels to one-star hostels. Before the coastline turns into the Bahia de Palma, a large indent of the shore forms the Playa de la Rapita and this is the site of another small hostel development, the Bris.

Palma de Mallorca

Few cities in the world mingle their Old World history with the present day so effectively as the cities of the Mediteranean. Few tiny cities of the Mediterranean are able to present both sides of their heritage so well and in such close proximity as Palma de Mallorca.

History mingles with modern life throughout this busy city of around 325,000 people. During the tourist season the population of Palma can swell to 500,000 as visitors come into the city from the many new hotels which are located along the shores of Palma Bay. Bikini-clad bathers take a dip in the waters which once hosted Roman slave galleys and mini-skirted tourists browse in markets where blacksmiths once provided military armour for the Crusaders. El Cid's hero, King Al-Mukadir, strolled the ramparts of Palma's citadel, the Amudaina Palace, where now the King of Spain often holds official functions, and Christopher Columbus possibly moored his merchant ship alongside a wharf now occupied by the latest design in cruising yacht technology.

Postcards from Palma de Mallorca often show visitors taking a leisurely ride along one of the city's tree-lined boulevards or along the promenade of the Paseo Maritimo in the local horse-drawn carriage known as a *galera*. This is by far the most comfortable way to view some parts of the Balearic Island's largest city. However, even though the entire central area of Palma is no more than 4km ($2^1/_2$ miles) across, there are many narrow streets, little lanes, stepped hillsides and hidden squares which are best explored on foot.

There are around fifty important sites of historic and cultural interest in the city if one includes the twenty or more churches and convents in the old part of Palma, but the average visitor's time to see the city's sights usually prevents intensive and prolonged tours. At least two full days in the city are required to take in the more important locations of old Palma.

It would also take twice as many days to discover modern Palma, its cafés, bars, entertainments and shopping facilities. However, the island's tourist board organises special half-day coach tours which take in the major sites of significance: the cathedral, the Lonja, Castle Bellver, the Almudaina Palace etc and some include organised shopping trips.

'When I took Mallorca from the Moors, it was the best thing that God willed a man to do in one hundred years past.' So wrote King Jaime I of Aragon in the Autumn of 1229 when he landed on the island not 15km (10 miles) south of the capital, Palma de Mallorca. He may well have made the same remark when he entered the city on the last day of that year and claimed it for Spain.

Prior to Jaime's arrival, the city of Palma had been ransacked in the Crusade of 1115 and the Moorish monuments of what the Arabs called *Medina Mayurka*, were destroyed. In those times the capital was a typical Arab garden city with date groves growing on the flat roofs of castellated mansions, wide canals where oared galleys moored in the busting docks and its skyline was pierced by the minarets of a hundred gleaming white, marble mosques.

Today that past granduer has been surpassed by almost eight centuries of architectural evolution. Practically no Moorish structures remain in Palma save the ancient Arab Baths and the occasional arabesque carving or tile built into more modern structures. The Crusaders took great delight in laying waste any evidence of Moorish occupation almost as much as they had enjoyed massacring the Arab inhabitants in retaliation for atrocities committed against the Christians. The great mosque that stood overlooking the extensive Bay of Palma was systematically torn down and the foundations of a great Christian cathedral were lain on the same spot.

It is this cathedral that greets the visitor, in towering gothic majesty, whichever way the traveller enters the city. It is said that the best way to view the city's famous sights is from the bay as one approaches the port by boat. Few visitors to Palma or Mallorca have this opportunity however, as most arrive at the Son Sant Juan International Airport to the east of the city.

Unless one is staying in the east of the island, at one of the many resorts to the south-east of Palma Bay, on the east coast or in the north (when a bypass of the city is generally taken) the convential route to the west, or to the city centre is via the wide highway from the airport. Here it meets the Autopista de Levante, or Ronda Litoral, just east of the city centre. This route eventually leads onto the Paseo Maritimo and around the curve of the harbour which Palma faces. Even from this grand esplanade several of the capital's greatest

Palma's La Seo Cathedral, with its huge flying buttresses and rose window, said to be the world's largest

Horse-drawn carriages await their passengers near the Almudaina Gardens in Palma

The Almudaina Palace, one of Palma's many historic buildings

historic monuments can be viewed.

It is the old part of Palma city which is of most interest to the visitor and this area is bounded to the south by the large port harbour, its long quay where cruise ships berth, terminating in its prominent lighthouse; to the east and north by an encircling road made up of a series of avenues named after famous grandees; and to the west by the Sa Riera Canal, bordered by the boulevard named the Paseo Mallorca. In this one square kilometre there are at least twenty famous historic sites.

The majestic monument of Palma's **La Seo Cathedral** founded in the reign of King Jaime I, in 1230, took three centuries to complete and a rebuilding of parts of the cathedral was necessary after an earthquake in 1851. Dominating the maritime parade and fronted by a large area known as the Parque de la Mar — the Sea Park — the dramatic sides of the great cathedral edifice rise up solid and fluted in Gothic splendour. This sight has drawn admiration from numerous literary figures including the French authoress George Sand who described the cathedral as 'an imposing mass, which rises from the sea'. The butressed flanks of this beige-coloured sandstone monument have been also likened to a 'great stone organ'. The western façade frames a huge rose window and its seaward side holds effigies of sages and notables of the Middle Ages. To the north side of the massive structure is the Almonia arched entrance and, facing south, great buttresses support the marvellous Portal del Mirador entrance designed by Guillem Sagrera, main architect of La Longa. The front entrance comprises of a 50ft high arch with vast double doors beneath a huge triangular gable. The tympanum contains a depiction of the Last Supper. Flying buttresses, gargoyles and intricate carvings lavish the whole, as icing on the most sumptuous of wedding cakes.

Inside, the cathedral's real beauty is breathtaking. The rose window, said to be the world's largest, throws light of pink and purple, golds, blues and mauves across the twin rows of seven narrow, freestanding columns which support the roof of the central nave. So slender and tall (up to 43.7m, 143ft) were the original columns, erected in 1368, and so heavy was the roof, that the columns began to bow, so, by the early 1600s, replacements were installed. Smaller stained glass rose windows echo the dramatic brilliance of the main window and shed their illumination down the two side naves. Thirty-two narrow windows in the walls glow with stained glass like jewelled arrow slits under soaring arches of simple, yet cleverly complicated design, a telling testament to the symetrical simplicity envisaged by its master builder, Pere Morey. The celebrated Catalan architect Antonio Gaudi was responsible for much of the later restoration work undertaken in 1904. From the central nave seventeen side chapels and treasure houses lead off, each with their own singular beauty. Included in the overall architectural plan of the cathedral are the Gothic chapter hall, the Baroque chapter hall, the Vermells sacristy, the eastern chapel of the Holy Trinity, built in 1276, and the Royal Chapel at the far end of the central of the three arches in the main nave. The honey-coloured stone from Santanyi in southeast Mallorca, used in the construction of the columns and the infilling of the pointed arches has given this basilica the name of 'the cathedral of light and space'.

Interior embellishments include the ancient high altar, the archbishop's chair, made in 1269, and the highly decorated, 110 choir stalls, carved in 1328. In the Royal Chapel repose the tombs of the two sovereigns, Jaime II and III (King Jaime I is buried in mainland Spain at Poblet). Renaissance tombs are set off by Gaudi's modern *baloquino*, a suspended sculpture of cloth, wire, paper and wood, hung over the main altar, and paintings, reliquaries, statues and reredos of various ages decorate the cathedral's chapels. The treasury contains thirteenth-century paintings, tapestries, gold and enamel work, silver candelabra, gem-studded crosses and more precious reliquaries.

The **Cathedral Museum** is housed in the Royal Palace, or Palau Reil, overlooking Palma's fine harbour across the Parque del Mar. As well as the opportunity to view the rare books, the magnificent St George and the Dragon reredos and a treasured statue of the Madonna, the view of Palma harbour from the stone gallery is a sight not to be missed. Shakespeare's seal and Louis XIV's silver mace are among the museum's most treasured exhibits. Part of this palace, the San Pablo Chapel, was built in the thirteenth century by Guillermo Sagrera, but the majority of the building dates from the seventeenth century and the year of the erection of the palace's façade is 1616. The sundial in the centre courtyard dates from 1734.

Adjacent to the palace building, on Miramar Street, are the exhibits of the **Majorca Church Museum**. These are housed in the Episcopal Palace, known as the Diocesan Museum. Here can be viewed medieval paintings, archaeological collections, ceramics and sculpture.

The **Palacio de Almudaina**, a fortress-like building which stands opposite the cathedral, was once a royal Moorish palace and continued to be the residence of the kings during the Middle Ages. Initially this was the site of a Roman citadel, which is what the Moorish name

Almudaina means. The Arab *Alcazar* on which the existing structure is built, was destroyed in the thirteenth century but the impressive ramparts, once part of the city's sea wall, was mostly constructed during the sixteenth century. The two archways bordering the patio date from Arab times and it is worth visiting the little Royal Chapel located behind a large wooden door in the King's Courtyard. Note the decorations on the underside of the arch and the angel on the palace's central tower. Much of this building, set around its square courtyard, is set aside as offices and the residences of visiting monarchs, including the Spanish Sovereignty. The **Museum of National Heritage** is housed in the Almudaina Palace and contains many interesting artifacts, magnificent furniture and glorious tapestries. This historic monument was mainly the work of Pere Salva who created the San Jaime and Santa Ana Chapels, the King and Queen's Palaces and the main meeting room.

It is necessary to cross the gardens of S'Hort del Rei, with its Moorish arch, noting, on the way, the Arab Pool set into the Ronda walls, crossing also the Avenida Antonio Maura to reach the next set of ancient monuments in the old city. On the Avenida Antonio Maura it is possible to hire either a taxi or a horse-drawn carriage (*galera*) to continue sightseeing further away from the harbour, but a walking tour of the sights is by far the best way to see historic Palma. Following the Paseo Sagrera (lined with palms — the tree from which the city takes its name) westwards on the right, the first main building is the **Museo Bellas Artes,** or Museum of Fine Art.

Just across from here, in the same block, is one of the world's most magnificent civil buildings, **La Lonja**. This castle-like building, Palma's ancient stock exchange, was also built by Sagrera between 1426 and 1450, and is probably his most famous work. As a Mediterranean trader in silks, it is possible that Christopher Columbus visited this exchange which, until about seventy years ago, was still used to store grain. Today, art exhibitions are frequently held in the magnificent Gothic edifice. Parts of the Lonja's turretted and castellated exterior look more befitting of a church, with its arched doorway, twin saint statues, gargoyles and embellished windows. Inside, two rows of six barleysugar-twist pillars hold up the vaulted roof and where they support the ceiling they form palm-like branches. Two spiral staircases lead to the roof, from which there is a glorious view of the harbour and portside buildings.

La Consolat del Mar, or Admiralty Court, stands back from La Loja, and is of significance for its seventeenth-century Renaissance gallery joining its five round pillars and the ceiling murals. There are

La Lonja, once Palma's stock exchange, where the young Columbus may have traded, is now used for art exhibitions

This art nouveau pastry shop contrasts with Palma's more ancient buildings

exhibits of maritime interest, charts and model ships in the foyer, but the main part of this building is now used by the Government of the Balearic Islands. Just to one side of this building are a few remains of fortified walls dating from the sixteenth century. Behind La Lonja is the fourteenth-century church of Santa Cruz, on the Puig de Sant Pere. Beneath the church is a thirteenth-century crypt.

Continuing westwards along the ancient city wall ruins, or the Bauarte de San Pedro, and turning right where the Paseo joins the Ronda Migjorn, one follows the Sa Riera canal to the Placa Porta de Santa Catalina. Cutting through the narrow streets towards the Plaza Pio XII, on Calle Zagranada is the Casa Colom with an eighteenth-century courtyard of particular significance. On San Cayetano, is the Casa Solleric, or **Solleric Art Museum**. On the way, on Calle Paz, on San Felio and on Montenegro are some famous seventeenth- and eighteenth-century mansions like Casa Weyler, Casa Belloto and Casa Montenegro. There are several more of these stately town houses like the Casa Margues on Apuntadores and the sixteenth-century Casa Oleza with its grand courtyard and balustraded staircase, on Cale Morey. On Calle San Cayetano is the exquisite Morell Palace which boasts one of the most attractive courtyards in Palma and a double stairway leading up to a magnificent gallery. The Casa Solleric is not far from one of the Tourist Board offices on Avenida Rey Jaime III. Running south from Plaza Pio XII is the celebrated boulevard known as the Paseo Des Born which leads to the Plaza de la Reina and back to the cathedral and the Almudaina Palace. Between the Avenue Rey Jaime III and the attractive *paseo* called La Rambla, or Via Roma, there are three of Palma's historic churches: San Jaime, Santa Magdelena and the Iglesia de la Conception.

From La Rambla head back into the old town by turning right. This leads to the **Theatro Principal** on Navarra and near to the Casa Berga, or law courts. This is just a few paces from the San Nicolas church. On the way to the cathedral the **Ayuntamiento**, or old town hall, on the bustling Plaza Cort, should be visited. This three-storied Renaissance structure is an excellent seventeenth-century example of Mallorcan architecture and houses an extensive portrait gallery and thousands of ancient documents, manuscripts and royal decrees dating back to the year before Jaime I took Palma. On Calle Almudaina, nearby, as well as the Arco de la Mar, or Arch of Almudaina, the 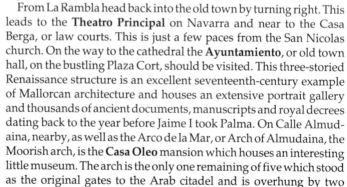 Moorish arch, is the **Casa Oleo** mansion which houses an interesting little museum. The arch is the only one remaining of five which stood as the original gates to the Arab citadel and is overhung by two ancient houses supported by moulded eaves. The house next to the arch-like bridge has an interesting bay window which looks as if it might have been adapted from a Moorish version. A short walk north leads to the Plaza Santa Eulalia and its ancient church. This is one of the oldest churches in Palma, being the first to be built after the Conquest, and was the site of the mass conversion of the Jews in 1435. It was up the steps of this church, and into the nave, that the scholar and poet, Ramon Llull, in about 1265, rode his charger in pursuit of a woman that had caught his fancy. According to legend when she showed him her diseased breasts he immediately took holy orders and became a monk. Continuing around the corner from Santa Eulalia is the Palacio Marques de Vivot which has a beautiful arched and columned courtyard.

Just a short distance from the palace is the famous church of San Fransisco and its attached convent. Fray Junipero Serra, founder of California, was a monk in the Fransican monastery here and his statue stands in front of the church. The St George and Dragon carving and the statue of the Virgin are two major features of the church's exterior. King Jaime I established a monastery on this site in 1232. Founded by King Jaime II in 1281, the Church of San Fransisco has a superb rose window and a fine Gothic interior which houses the tomb of Ramon Llull, the great Mallorcan poet and scholar. His statue stands in one of the five side chapels and he is buried in an alabaster sarcophagus in the small chapel of Our Lady of Consolation located behind the high altar.

On Calle Ramon Llull, around the corner from Plaza San Fransisco are the **Archives of the Kingdom of Mallorca**, containing many fascinating documents dealing with the history of this area of the Mediterranean. In the block across the Plaza from the Church of San Fransisco, is the sixteenth-century **Casa Marques de Palmer**, on Calle Sol. This is probably the most notable of Palma's numerous city mansions and its main feature is the façade in a style which developed in this city between the sixteenth and seventeenth centuries. At the end of Calle Sol is the Plaza del Temple and the El Temple church which used to be the site of a Knights Templar castle, the remains of which can be seen in the oratory.

Down the Pont y Vich P Nadal, towards the harbour, is the **Museo de Mallorca**, on Calle Portella at Ca La Gran Cristiana Arqueologia. The museum is housed in the seventeenth-century palace of the Counts of Ayamans and has exhibits of many medieval paintings, altar pieces, sculptures, Moorish ceramics and early artifacts. Just off the sea esplanade, behind the Museum of Mallorca is the **Arab Baths**, one of the only complete surviving Arab structures in Mallorca. Inside this ancient, dilapidated monument, twelve columns, which are thought to be Roman, support Normanesque arches leading into two main chambers. These are known as the *calderium*, used for steam bathing, and the *tepiderium*, where rich Arabs took their cold baths much as one does in a sauna today.

A few strides away is the Convent of Santa Clara with a Baroque entrance, eighteenth-century frontage and thirteenth-century cloisters. The Baroque style church of Montesion on the block alongside Calle Viento (Windy Street), contains a sixteenth-century carved reredos although the church itself dates from a century later. If one walks south from Montesion down Amor Escuelas and Calle Berard the harbourside is reached. Plaza Llorenc faces the wide Parc de la Mar, or Park of the Sea and Palma Bay. It is now only a short walk to the cathedral to the west and the boulevard of Avenida Gabriel Alomar Villalonga to the east. By following the remains of the city wall, the Murallas, to Avenida Villalonga and walking a few paces to the Plaza Porta d'es Camp, there is a bus station from where you can get to most parts of the city.

Motorised transport is needed to reach several other historic monuments which lie further out from the centre of Palma. However, it is possible to walk about seven blocks east from the bus station in Avenida Villalonga to the **Museo Krekovic** and its artistic collection. A good distance west, past the fishing harbour and on the other side of the Sa Riera canal, the Paseo Mallorca and Avenida de la Argentina, is a famous cluster of ancient windmills known as Es Jonquet. At least six almost intact round-towered mills stand like sentinels overlooking the Nautical Club in the bay and reminiscent of those which challenged Don Quixote in Cervantes' famous novel.

Set high on a green hill at the west side of the Bay of Palma is the grand **Castillo Bellver**. It is a good drive from the centre of the city to the fourteenth-century castle, which is a masterpiece of Gothic architecture and features a unique circular courtyard at its heart. Three semi-circular turrets flank the rotund interior bastion and a great tower dominates the entire structure which is surrounded by an almost cloverleaf secondary ring of ramparts. A moat encircles the excellently preserved fort whose name means 'beautiful view'. However, it was not for the view that King Jaime II instructed architect Pere Salva to build his home here. He expected another raid by the Moorish invaders but, after a succession of royal occupations, in 1408, the keys of the castle were handed over to the prior of the Carthusian monks of Valldemossa. In 1717 the world's most impor-

Nets and boats in Palma's fishing harbour

The resorts around Andraitx, southwest of Palma, are quieter than those nearer the capital

tant medieval castle passed back into the hands of the Spanish Crown. Today Castillo Bellver houses a museum with artifacts dating back to Roman times and the grounds in which it stands is now a public park.

From the top of Bellver Castle can be seen another grand fortress, Castillo de Bendinat which stands in grounds overlooking a golf course. It was built by King Jaime II's father, Jaime I, but the present building dates only from the eighteenth century. Just one other monument of historic interest lies to the north-west of the city centre, on Calle Capitan Mesquida Veny. This is the **Peublo Español**, or Spanish Village, which is a collection of various types of Spanish house, palace and monument architecture faithfully reproduced to show the development of building styles.

Past the Spanish Village at the end of Calle Andrea Doria is the village of **Genova**, one of the places claiming to be the birthplace of Christopher Columbus. Nearby are the Genova Caves, and while the limestone formations are nowhere as spectacular as the caves of Drach or Hams on the island's east coast, they are the nearest caves to the Mallorcan capital.

Modern Palma, encircling a flotilla of sailing craft from luxurious yachts to humble fishing boats, rims the Bay of Palma and extends up the tree-covered hillside from palm-lined boulevards and magnificent historic edifices lining the maritime esplanade. To the north of the old city is the railway station FFCC Soller. This provides rail transport not only to Soller, but also to Inca, and also includes the main bus station from which almost every point of the island of Mallorca can be reached.

While in this area it is worth heading south from the main train and bus station to the indoor market in Plaza del Olivar. Here can be seen all manner of fruit, vegetables, meat and fish, the latter in particular showing the rich and varied harvest from the warm sea around the island.

North of the railway station is the Plaza de Toros, or bull ring. On the northern limits of the city are the dogtrack, the sports arena and football stadium, all of which lie outside the series of avenues and streets which encompass the main city centre.

Intermingled with numerous historic landmarks, the city centre bubbles with modern-day life, restaurants, cafés, bars, discotheques, nightclubs, cinemas, playhouses, theatres, concert halls, strip joints, art galleries, shops of every kind and a plethora of bazaars and markets, jostle for space on some of the city's tiny alleyways or wide boulevards. This is the city of art and culture during the day and excitement and stimulation at night. The city of Palma de Mallorca rarely seems to sleep, and if it is caught having a short siesta, there are always the attractions of nearby hotels and beach resorts or the clean, fresh, aromatic air of the Mallorcan countryside.

ACCOMMODATION IN PALMA DE MALLORCA

Palma de Mallorca, as the Balearic's capital city, has more hotels than any other location, with more than fifty hotels and residential apartments ranging from five-star to one-star ratings. The city has over sixty hostels and other accommodations. The Hotel Victoria Sol is listed as a five-star establishment and is located below the Castillo Bellver to the west side of the city. The Son Vida Sheraton Hotel is the most outstanding four-star establishment located to the city's north west, and others of the same rating include the Melia Victoria and the Valparaiso Palace. The Bellver-Sol, the Nixe Palace on the city outskirts, Iberotel Uto Palma, Palas Atenea-Sol and the Racquet Club are all four-star hotels.

Of the twenty or so three-star establishments in Palma several are residential hotels and apartments. Among the leading hotels of this rating the Rembrant, the Costa Azul, the Saratoga Hotel, the Jaime III Sol and the Drach are representative. Others of the same rating include the Araxa, Bosque Sol, Club Nautico, The Mirador, Palladium, La Caleta, The Nacar, Apartsuite and La Almudaina. Two-star establishments include The Cannes, El Paso, Rex, Rosamar and The Isla Mallorca hotel.

Mallorca — The South and West

This section encompasses the Calvia peninsula south-west of Palma and from the Isle of Dragonera in the extreme south-west to the Castillo del Rey in the far north. It includes numerous famous resorts, rocky bays, cliff-top beauty spots, sandy coves and the grand, mountain scenery of the Tramontana range.

This journey includes the only private railway in Spain — the Palma to Soller route — the popular resorts on Palma's outskirts and the Caliva beach complexes. In contrast it includes the lesser-known mountain and coastal beauty spots of the Sierra de Tramontana and Sierra de San Vicente, where the traveller will find an ancient castle, grand landscaped villas and palaces, lonely monasteries and ruined convents of great historical interest.

The main boulevard along the harbourside of Palma de Mallorca is no new sight to the millions of visitors who have travelled past its cathedral, hillside windmills, tower apartments and magnificent

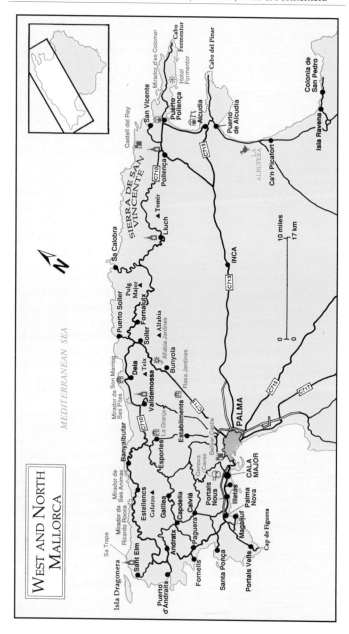

Bellver Castle to reach their holiday accommodation on the western arm of the great Bahia de Palma. It is after seeing Palma's mixture of ancient and modern architecture and then viewing the port when passing the twin fifteenth-century towers of Pelaires at **Porto Pi**, that the visitor begins to realise what a complex island Mallorca is.

Prickly pears protrude from honey-coloured ancient walls, sunlight bounces in dazzling brilliance off high hotel blocks and olive terraces begin to appear, speckled with dark cypress trees. All this is reflected in the limpid waters of the bay until the highway cuts inland, bypassing the rocky resort of Cala Major and the stylish hotels of Ca's Catala.

Continuing along the freeway, and up on the tree-clad hillside, the visitor will notice the impressive Castle of Bendinat, where King Jaime I remarked on the excellence of Mallorcan food in the early thirteenth century. In its shadow is a modern golf course. Beyond the golf course is the small resort of Illetes and here the *autopista* reaches the western outskirts of **Portals Nous** (New Arches), named after the area's sea caves. In the parish church on the beachfront at Portals Nous the statue of the 'Wandering Virgin' can be seen.

After a busy interjunction on the highway, to the left, can be seen the resort of Costa d'en Balnes, a dolphinarium and marina. Soon, after the Puerto Portals complex, the highway reaches the well known resort areas of **Palma Nova** and **Magalluf**, gateways to the Santa Ponça peninsula. Heading south from Palma Nova, a short secondary road leads to the Poniente golf course, Sa Porrassa sports centre, the yacht harbours of Sol de Mallorca and El Toro, the village of Portals Vells and the headland of Cap de Cala Figuera, Palma Bay's westernmost point. **Portals Vells** is famous for its cave of Our Lady located to the right of the cove. A cleft in the rocky shoreline contains a statue of the Virgin, placed here by thankful Genoese sailors who survived a storm off this coast.

However, continuing west is the **Coll de la Batalla** (King Jaime I's initial battle site in 1229), and the altarstone of Piedra Sagrada, connected with the same event. Here there is a small oratory on the site of where the first mass on the island was held, erected on the seven hundreth anniversary of the conquest in September 1929. On this road to Santa Ponça also is an iron cross commemorating those killed in the battle for succession of the island.

At the roundabout on the Andraitx road, keep the windmill immediately to your right unless you want to visit the beach resort of **Santa Ponça** with its marina and golf course. Near the Yacht basin of Sa Caleta is the Santa Ponça white cross where the Catalan conqueror, King Jaime I landed. The cross, carved by sculptor Tomas Vila, was erected in 1929. Near the town is the castle-style stately home of Santa Ponça and Es Castellot, a fortified watchtower built in 1769, during the reign of King Pedro IV of Aragon, to guard against the pirates then active on this coastline.

In the opposite direction to the many-hotelled town of Santa Ponça, and keeping the roundabout windmill to your left, a short drive takes the visitor to the 'Lamb and Flag' town of **Calvia**, the municipal centre of the area. An alternative excursion when visiting Calvia is to combine a trip to the town's parish church of San Sebastian, where the ornate façade is the work of local sculptor Biel Lliset, with a tour to the prehistoric *talayot* of Tora perched on its mountain top. Few visitors take this detour but it is useful to note, if you are based in a resort on the Costa Calvia, that the weekly market here is held each Monday morning. To the west of Calvia is the pretty little village of **Capdella**.

If one keeps to the road which skirts the Costa Calma part of the Calvia Peninsula, the last resort of this important municipality is Cala Fornells and the town of **Peguera**. Although there is an *autopista* which cuts down the distance between Palma and Peguera the resorts of this region are among the best known of all tourist attractions on the island — Illetes, Portals Nous, Puerto Portals, the Costa d'en Blanes, Palma Nova, Magaluf, Santa Ponça, Cala Fornells and Peguera.

After leaving the Calvia municipality and just before the little inlet of Camp de Mar, and after Cabo Andritxol, the highway turns inland to the ancient town of **Andraitx**, known in Roman times as *Andrachium*. The town itself lies at the centre of this westernmost peninsula of Mallorca and the resort village of Port d'Andraitx is situated on the coast south of the town. Andraitx was once fortified and one of its old turrets still stands. Medieval narrow cobbled streets wind between red-tiled, rust-brown houses, some of which probably date back to when the church was re-built in 1720. The church foundation is, however, much older and some historians date it as early as the thirteenth century, around the time of King Jaime I's landing. This may well have been the first proper church built on the island after Moorish occupation. The Bishop of Barcelona was given the land on which the town stands by Jaime in 1232. Subsequently Mallorcan bishops ruled here and there has been a Barony of Andraitx from then until 1811. The tower and mansion of Son Mas in Andraitx was constructed in the sixteenth century. It is locally known as the Torre de 'Sagrament'. In 1578 this tower was attacked by the Moors and a local hero, celebrated in a painting in the church, a Captain Fransisco Desmas, defended the tower thus preventing the invasion of Andraitx. A colourful open-air market is held in Andraitx on Wednesdays.

Port d'Andraitx is a small sheltered port now popular with the yachting fraternity, and resort hotels ring this almost full-moon shaped cove. The romanesque hermitage on the farm of Son Orlandis outside Port d'Andraitx was constructed in 1935 but the farm and its estate are much older.

There is little development along the coast westwards from Port d'Andraitx but a number of tiny coves and inlets can be explored by boat. The village of **Sant Elm** (or San Telmo) is the furthest west of any settlement on Mallorca. This village is named after St Elmo, the patron saint of mariners, who is best known for 'St Elmo's fire' — the luminous electrical discharge which can sometimes appear on ships during a storm. Sant Elm is famous for its historical connections, particularly the church and hospital founded in 1279 by King Jaime II and the tower of San Telmo built in 1531 as a defence watchtower for Andraitx and once owned by the Archduke Louis Salvador of Austria in 1886. From San Telmo one can view, or even take a boat trip out to the rugged island of **Dragonera**. The other, tiny islet seen from Sant Elm is Pantaleu, where Jaime I first set foot on Mallorca. Dragonera, however, has a small harbour with a few houses and three lighthouses because of the notoriously turbulent sea in this part of Mallorca's waters. The island is an important wildlife and birdlife sanctuary and is now protected by the Grupo Ornithologico Balear. To the north of Sant Elm is Mallorca's most western cape, **Cabo Tramontana**, and one should not miss a visit to the ancient ruined convent of Sa Trapa.

Between San Telmo and Andraitx is the settlement of S'Arraco which developed from an estate on the site established in the eighteenth-century, and the chapel of Santo Cristo. The region became a parish including Sa Trapa, Sa Palomera and San Telm valleys in 1849. Inland and north of Andraitx, Puig Punent village, the orchards around Galilea and the seventeenth-century Son Forteza are all worth an excursion before leaving this part of south-western Mallorca.

There are five main roads out of Andraitx, to Palma via Paguera, to Porto Andraitx, west to Sant Elm, north to Puig Punent and north-west, the C710 road which heads up the western side of the Tramontana mountains towards Valldemossa. The first landmarks on this winding coastal road is the *mirador*, or lookout point of Ses

Shady balconies surrounded by a covered veranda are a feature of Mallorca's many old country mansions, as here at La Granja

The bust of Archduke Salvador of Austria, in the museum at the monastery at Valldemossa

Ortiques with its view of numerous sea-locked coves and magnificent cliffs and then Mirador Ricardo Rocca, after which the road runs
through a short tunnel. A little further on is the orchard-surrounded
town of **Estellencs** clinging to the slopes of Mount Galatzo in a
landscape dotted with lovely old farms and country villas. Estellencs
has a picturesque church with a sundial built into its bell tower.
There are two ancient round watchtowers a short distance along the
cliff-top road. These were built between the fifteenth and seven-

*There is a magnificent view of the north-west coast of Mallorca from
Son Marriog*

teenth centuries and the Estellencs tower is known as the Atalaya de Ses Animas — the ' Tower of Souls'. Sometimes called the ' Tower of Owls', this fine viewpoint is reached by a little stone bridge. It is possible to take a precarious track down to Cala de Estellencs, a tiny cove surrounded by cliffs.

Back on the main road the next township is the terraced settlement of **Banyalbufar** looking seaward from its mountainside perch. The whole countryside is also terraced and this area was once famous for its Melvoise wine made from grapes grown on the 'Madeiraesque' slopes. The road winds inland from the ragged coast after Banyalbufar and continues north and inland to the large town of Valdemossa, but a return can be made to Palma by taking a right turn just after Banyalbufar, running through the hamlets of Esporles and Establiments. This road passes the stalely country house or *finca* of La Granja, where visitors can see furnishings from the seventeenth and eighteenth centuries as well as numerous artifacts.

Valldemossa lies in the north-east of the island, at the foot of Mount Teix, and was visited by the celebrated missionary Ramon Llull in the early fourteenth century and by Archduke Louis Salvador of Austria in 1872. Robert Graves' house on Mallorca is located here and Valldemossa is the birthplace of the island's saint, Catalina Thomas. Her body is preserved intact in Palma and, in the village, the saint's house is open to visitors. The Gothic church nearby dates from 1245, and contains a statue of Saint Catalina.

King Sancho set up court at Valldemossa in 1311 and King Martin, in 1339, gave Sancho's palace to the Carthusian monks who were expelled from Spain in 1835. The Carthusian monastery, known as La Real Cartuja, and its nunnery at San Bruno, where there is now a small museum, was founded by the Catalan King Martin the Humane, and rebuilt by monks in the eighteenth century. This building has been home to travelling visitors such as Frederick Chopin, George Sand and famous painters. Mementos of Chopin and Sand, who stayed at the monastery during 1838-9, include the former's piano, scores and death-mask. Their apartment 'cells' can be visited and some of the frescoes in the monastery are by Goya's brother-in-law, Manuel Bayeu. An eighteenth-century pharmacy museum nearby has interesting exhibits of early medicinal containers.

High on the road overlooking the sea is the stone lookout called King Jaime's Chair, a stone throne near the summit of Teix mountain. This is a beauty spot enjoyed by the king who believed that the thin air relieved his asthmatic condition.

However, it was King Sancho, Jaime's successor, who built the

castle at Valldemossa and who was the actual asthm[...]
Mallorca! Local farms of importance include Sa Coma a[...]
both once owned by the Archduke Salvador of Austri[...]

Heading towards Soller several interesting farmstea[...]
manor houses are passed on the road, while to the left can be seen[...]
balcony viewpoint known as the Mirador de Ses Pites with its two-
storey watchtower, dating from 1606.

This is the Miramar coastline so loved by the Archduke Salvador,
who bought a good part of this coastline and its properties. Near this
mirador, or viewpoint, is the cave where Ramon Llull lived and wrote
and from where he established the first western college for Arab
studies. The chapel nearby dates from 1876 and Son Gallard farm
was once home of Saint Catalina. Son Marroig manor, a little further
along to the left of the Soller road, was one of the Archduke Salvador's favourite residences and is open to visitors. Below here is the
crag of Sa Foradada ('perforated rock'). In prehistoric times the
waves bored a hole in a great craggy outcrop of rock jutting out into
the sea. This headland is known as the Punta de Sa Foradada. The
pinnacle of this cliff is higher than Palma cathedral's spire. The road
follows this rugged coastline down into the pretty village of **Deia**
with its narrow cobbled streets. It is popular with writers and artists
and there is a small archaeological museum. At Lluch Alcari the road
heads inland to the town of Soller.

Soller nestles in a neat valley in the shadow of the 1,445m (4,741ft)
mountain, Puig Mayor. The Moors named the town *Sulliar*, the
'Golden Shell', because to them it was a precious gem. It claims,
amongst many other places on Mallorca, to be the birthplace of
Christopher Columbus. The entrance to the town, through the
Avenida de Soller is most picturesque.

Soller had, and still has, much to offer in trade and tourism. The
area is well known as a centre for orange and lemon groves and the
local market attracts buyers and sellers of fruit and vegetables every
Saturday morning. Soller contains several interesting buildings and
relics such as its ancient church which boasts an Italian sculpted
black marble statue of St Bartholome, the town's patron saint, and a
carved Madonna which dates from the fourteenth century. The
façade of the tall-spired church is late nineteenth century and is built
in the art nouveau style. The Soller House of culture is located on
Calle del Mar and contains an interesting collection of artifacts.

Soller town is encompassed by two mountain ridges and was once
practically inaccessible. For centuries a stage coach ran the hazardous journey over tortuous mountain passes from Palma de Mallorca.

The electric tram is a popular way of travelling between Puerto Soller and Soller

The seafront at Puerto Soller

Fornalutx, with its steep cobbled streets, is regarded as one of the most picturesqe villages on Mallorca

A weathered wooden door leads into a cool hallway in Fornalutx

As Soller became more important there was a need to reduce the isolation of the town from the rest of the island, caused by the Sierra Norte. So at the turn of the twentieth century a railway was planned. The problem with constructing a railway from Palma de Mallorca to link with Soller was the Sierra Norte, the Northern Mountains, which stood in the way. After careful planning and almost six years of work, tunnels were excavated through the range and a private company built the narrow-gauge railway through thirteen mountains and hills to connect Palma with Soller. The longest of the tunnels is almost 3km long (nearly 2 miles), and the total distance is 27km (17 miles). Inaugurated in 1905, planned the next year and opened in 1912 the railway brought Soller's early tourists to its sites of antiquity, its little El Guia hotel near to the rail station and the town's well-loved Saturday morning market. A tram system was constructed to connect Soller town with the coast at **Puerto Soller**, a distance of 5km (3 miles), using tramcars said to have been imported from San Fransisco. On the main Palma to Soller line electric engines replaced steam trains in 1929.

Today, the Palma to Soller train service is the only privately run line in the whole of Spain. The hour-long journey goes through dramatic scenery, but the train's seating is basic and not very comfortable and it can be very chilly in the tunnels.

Elsewhere on the island there once was a rail link from Palma to Santanyi in the south-east, while the line which now only runs between Palma and Inca once had branch lines to the towns of Felantix in the east, Artá via Manacor in the north-east, and La Puebla in the north. A bus service now provides these links which the rail system has abandoned.

Leaving Soller for Palma the road climbs innumerable hairpins over the Soller Pass at about 914m (3,000ft) and then snakes down to the orchard-filled plains. Landscaped gardens are an attraction along the route to Palma and these are well worth the diversion off the road. **Bunyola** is a tiny hamlet with a market on Saturday mornings and a grand house of the same name with landscaped lands, to the east of the rail route and although it cannot be visited it is an important landmark. Raxa is another sumptuous villa with Italianesque architecture dating from the late sixteenth century. The Alfabia Jardines to the east side of the Soller road is another example of countryside exhuberance, with landscaped gardens to visit. However it is the natural beauty of the region that makes a lasting impression, such as the steep wild slopes of the Sierra de Alfabia and the peak of Alfabia which rises to a height of 1,068m (3,500ft) and can be seen to the east of the railway as it approaches Soller.

From Puerto Soller on the coast one must back-track to Soller itself to join the road which winds its way north into the Siera de Torrellas. Apart from the Monastery of Lluc, the main attraction on this route is the spectacular scenery — among the best on the island. Indeed, the Lluch road leads through mountain passes to Pollença and the coast at Puerto Pollença.

Just out of Soller on the C710 road to Lluch the pretty villages of **Fornalutx** and **Bibiaraix** nestle in an area covered with citrus and almond groves. The next stop is the Mirador Ses Barques, 'ship's lookout', high above the ultramarine Mediterranean. At 1,445m (4,740ft) Puig Mayor, the highest peak on the island, with its distinctive early warning system domes, cannot be missed to the left . The lake to the right is the Cuber reservoir, popular with ornithologists. At the Comasema farmhouse, one can take a stroll in this wild and dramatic scenery.

However, back on the Lluch road the next feature passed is the Gorg Blau dam from which one can reach the remote resort beaches beneath the steep cliffs at **Sa Calobra** and Cala Tuent. The road down to the sea here is steep and narrow with sheer drops and there is also coaches or lorries to be wary of. At one point to lose height quickly the road loops underneath itself. This road is not for the timid. The twin water shoots of Sa Torrente de Pareis at Sa Calobra, as the river bounds down a steep, rocky gorge into the narrow inlet, must be one of Mallorca's most famous natural spectacles.

Back to the main road the C710 leads to **Lluch** — one of the most devoutly religious places on the island with many stories of the 'Morenata', or Brown Virgin, such as her lost crown recovered from the sea by fishermen, or the seventh-century vision of the Virgin seen in the sky at Lluch. The monastery of Lluch is at 400m (1,300ft), high up in the mountains and 11 miles west of Inca town. Here is the sanctuary of the Virgin of Lluch, patron saint of Mallorca. The Augustinian monastery at Lluch was originally built in the seventh century at Escora, about 4km (2½ miles) west of its present site, and was called the Chapel of San Pedro, where there is a fine lookout. However, the monastic building just outside Lluch itself, was built in 1430. Lluch means the 'sacred forest' and this site has such a pull that over 50,000 pilgrims visit the religious centre and, for less devout visitors, the museum here has a most interesting collection of antiques, religious gifts, and sundry items loosely connected with the miracles.

From the monastery the main road again winds north passing the

The road to Sa Calobra winds down through the mountains to the coast

The Augustinian monastery of Lluch

1,103m (3,619ft) Puig Tomir on the right to sweep down into the town of Pollença. To the left of the road as one drives into Pollença is the great divide of the San Vicente mountain range covering the far north-west flank of this part of the island. The most prominent man-made feature of the Sierra San Vicente is the ruin of Castell del Rey, or the Castle of the King, on the clifftop reached either by a small road from Pollença, or from the village of San Vicente, north of Pollença. The castle was a Moorish fort, rebuilt by King Jaime I in the twelfth century, maintained against a seige from the mainland by King Jaime II in 1285, and captured only once in 1343. The fortress stands more than 460m (1,500ft) above the swirling waves and currents of the cliffs near Punta Galera. **Cala San Vicente** is a cove nearby often visited from Pollença.

Pollença and Alcúdia

Although Pollença does not constitute one of Mallorca's largest townships the Polleça and Alcúdia region in the far north of the island attracts a great many visitors, as it includes the resorts of

Puerto de Pollença, Formentor and Alcúdia. Alcúdia Bay also has the longest beach in Mallorca and the ancient walled town is a particular attraction for visitors to the island.

One of the most visited and interesting of Mallorca's towns, **Pollença** lies in the north-east of the island just off the road from Palma de Mallorca to the Formentor peninsula. A little inland from its sister town of Puerto Pollença on the north coast, Pollença itself has a population of almost 13,000 and lies in a valley area between the Puig, or Peak of Pollença, the Puig Tomir, and the range of the Sierra de Tramuntana mountains.

Surrounded by agricultural land and orchards, Pollença is set on the Torrente Sant Jordi River which can be no more than a stream at times but is spanned by a famous Roman bridge. The bridge, *Puente Romana*, testifys to the town's ancient roots although experts suggest that it was actually constructed by the Arabs in the early thirteenth century. Remains have been found which suggest that the site of Pollença dates from the Bronze Age and its name is taken from the name the Romans gave to nearby Alcudia — *Pollentia*. Certainly this quiet town has had a varied history and it was a Knights Templar stronghold after Moorish rule until 1312, and a Knights Hospitaler citadel until 1802. The celebrated Moros y Cristianos annual August re-enactment of the fights between the Moors and Christians maintains the traditions of the town's ancestry.

This event is Pollença's fiesta, while the town's other annual event is the more modern Pollença Music Festival, begun in 1962 and held in the cloisters of the Sant Domingo Convent during July and August. These two events attract a great number of tourists from all over the island. Two English connections with the town are Philip Newman who inaugurated the festival and the crime writer Agatha Christie who set one of her books in Pollença. On Sunday mornings people come from the tourist resorts on the coast and the surrounding area to the weekly market in the town centre.

Among the town's historic buildings is the Calvari, a tiny eighteenth-century chapel reached by the 365 steps of the picturesque 'Calvary Stairway' or Calvario. Before climbing the cypress-lined steps look for the cockerel-topped fountain guarding the stairs. The sanctuary at the summit contains a crucifix which supposedly arrived there by some miraculous act. From the hermitage here one can see across to Puerto Pollença and the sea in the north and to the hilltop sanctuary of the convent chapel on Puig Maria.

Back in the main part of Pollença, the great barrel-vaulted Baroque cathedral, the Parroguia, dominates the Plaza Major. Nearby is the

Convento de San Domingo, now housing the municipal museum and the location for the annual music concert. San Domingo was built in 1578, twenty-seven years after Pollença was attacked by the pirate Dragut who was repulsed by the local hero Joan Farragut, and its cloisters are of architectural significance. A number of grand historic town houses can be seen along Calle Jesus and around the plaza and some of Pollença's other attractions include the fifteenth-century Gothic, Roser Vell oratorio and chapel, the church of Sant Jordi, the church of Montision, and the eighteenth-century town hall. Although application must be made in writing, the Collection Costa y Llobera may be of interest to historians of local culture and art.

Places to visit within easy striking distance of Pollença include the caves of San Vicente and a tour of the Formentor peninsula where there are several *miradors*, or viewpoints.

A short distance north from Pollença brings the visitor to the popular harbour of **Puerto Pollença**, protected by two peninsulas of land. This little fishing port has become a great tourist attraction but has retained its identity among the hotels, restaurants, bars and stores which line its quayside. Artists flock to this pretty village which has been given the accolade of being one of the best bays in the Mediterranean. An attractive promenade lined with palms and pine trees runs from the centre of the resort around the north side of the bay, and offers shade from the summer's heat. Several eccentric foreigners have made this their home, one in particular has built himself a 'castle' just outside the village in the mountains and, shopping in Pollença in his donkey-drawn 'charriot', has become one of the local personalities.

There are a dozen or so art galleries and antique shops to browse through in Puerto Pollença and the Anglada Museum has a good collection of paintings by the celebrated artist Anglada Camarasa whose works date from the early twentieth century. The village holds its weekly market every Wednesday morning in the little square near the church. Sporting facilities around Puerto Pollença include all forms of watersports, tennis, horse riding and a nine-hole golf course. Boat trips can be made from here and walking visits might include some of the beautiful bays and sights of this region such as those of Boquer, Figuera, San Vicente, Ternells, Castell Bay and its Moorish castle, the lighthouse or *faro* at Formentor and the L'Atalaia d'Alberteutx.

The Bay of Pollença is formed by two north-pointing peninsulas, Cape Pinar to the east and **Cape Formentor** to the west. Huge cliffs, some 200m (650ft) in height, tower above spectacular sandy bays and

A relaxing cup of coffee in the Plaza Major, Pollença

The yacht harbour at Puerto Pollença

Puerto Pollença's attractive tree-lined promenade

little coves. One such cove lies a short distance north of Puerto Pollença, the Cala de la Pi de la Posada, site of the famous Formentor Hotel, haunt of the rich and famous including film stars, royalty and politicians. This hotel is the oldest and most respected on Mallorca, dating from 1926. There is a regular ferry service from Puerto Pollença which takes visitors to the beach here, and backed by pine trees offers pleasant shade.

On the opposite side of the peninsula from the hotel and Playa Formentor, but also reached by road from Puerto Pollença, is the Mirador d'es Colomer, overlooking the tiny islet of Colomer. The viewpoint is splendidly engineered on a sheer, overhanging cliff to give marvellous views of the sea hundreds of feet below. As this is a popular attraction for coach tours of the island it is likely to be crowded, but despite this it should not be missed. For the energetic a stiff climb up a track opposite the *mirador* leads to the old watch-tower of Albercutx, which gives superb views of Formentor and the Bay of Pollença.

Once past the Hotel Formentor the road surface deteriorates until after about 11km (7 miles) of narrow and steep road with sheer drops, the most northerly point of the island is reached. Here at Cabo Formentor is just a lighthouse and a tiny souvenir shop.

From the peninsula of Formentor the main road sweeps around the Pollença Bay in a great arc past Puerto Pollença, to the great *murallas*, or city walls of the ancient town of **Alcúdia** .

Like many other towns on the island (eg Pollença, Andraitx, Soller), Alcúdia was built several miles inland of its port to protect the population from marauding pirates who roamed the Mediterra-nean. Originally a Phoenician settlement, a Greek and then a Roman port of great significance from the second century BC up to its destruction by the Vandals in the sixth century AD, this historic town has evidence of its history in the many Roman remains here. Alcúdia was founded in 123BC by the Roman general Quinto Cecilio Metelo and the original site has been excavated near the church of San Jaime, across the road which skirts the town walls. Here can be seen streets and columns, as well as the foundations and walls of buildings. The Romans named Alcúdia *Pollentia*, which somehow was used by the neighbouring settlement, and a Roman wall skirts the town together with one constructed in Medieval times. Apart from Palma de Mallorca, Alcúdia has more monuments and buildings of historic and archaeological interest than any other of the island's towns. Indeed the contrasts between ancient and modern in the region is remarkable as tourists in brightly coloured outfits stroll through sombre ancient alleyways or gaze in awe at the great Roman remains and medieval gateways.

The oldest standing monument in the region is the smallest Greco-Roman amphitheatre in the whole of Spain and dates from the first century BC. The amphitheatre may be visited and is located a mile outside the town just off the road to Puerto Alcúdia. It was excavated in 1953, and as well as the tiers of seats there is a changing room excavated in the rock. Two paleochristian chapels, the 'Saint Martin's Cave' are located outside the town and the twin altars here are dedicated to St Martin and St George.

The ancient Jara, or Xara Gate, was built in the fifteenth century and is one of only two original gates remaining in the Roman and Medieval walls. It leads out to the east and to the harbour of Puerto Alcúdia. The other gate, Puerta de San Sebastian, was also constructed in the fifteenth century and leads to the west. On the way to the harbourside can be seen the Chapel of Santa Ana which dates from the thirteenth century. This little church, built on the site of ancient *Pollentia*, was once a hermitage, and is a fine example of early Mallorcan Gothic ecclesiastical architecture.

The magnificent high wall which surrounds Alcúdia with its square, castellated towers, protects the ancient town's narrow streets lined with beautiful sixteenth- and seventeenth-century houses sporting Gothic doorways and fascinating architectural embellishments. One of the houses on Calle de Roca is even said to have sheltered Charlemagne on his visit to Mallorca in the eighth century. Other notable manor houses in the town include that on Calle Barri; the Renaissance structures of Ca'n Amoros; the sixteenth-century windows of the houses of Carrer de's Moll; those of Casa Viver on Calle Roca and those on the corner of Calle Marques de Zayas in the Ca'n Fondo; Calle Serra's eighteenth-century mansions and the seventeenth-century edifice of Ca'n Costa on the Calle San Vicente; the house on Calle Bennassar and the seventeenth-century Casa Busquets on Calle Valients; the ancient museum of C'an Domenech on Cale General Goded and the fifteenth-century house on Calle Damien Ramis. The archaeological museum on Calle San Jaime, founded in 1948 by the Bryant Foundation, houses some interesting mosaics, bronzes and statues from Alcúdia's chequered past. The old parish church of Alcúdia was constructed in 1302 and is dedicated to St James, the town's patron saint. The town hall by stark comparison, is recent as it was built in 1929.

Today bull fights are a great tourist attraction in the town and there is an excellent market held here every Sunday. Mallorca's islanders

There are marvellous view from the Mirador d'es Colomar, on an overhanging cliff hundreds of feet above the sea

⇐ The scenery at Cape Formentor is both rugged and dramatic

Street entertainers in Alcúdia add interest and colour

The fifteenth-century Jara Gate in Alcúdia

refer to Alcúdia as 'capertown' for the fine capers grown in the region, but visitors know it better for the spectacular 15km (9 mile) sandy beach — the longest on the island — and the harbour of Puerto de Alcúdia just outside the town.

On the north side of the Alcúdia town walls, two roads lead out to the wild Alcúdia peninsula. The Sanctuary of La Ermita Victoria stands towards the tip of the headland, Cabo Pinar (or cape of pines), near an ancient watchtower, and was originally constructed in the thirteenth century, but rebuilt during the seventeenth century. The watchtower itself, Torre Mayor, was built by order of King Philip II in 1599.

Generally packed with yachts, dinghies and all manner of craft including the daily ferry to Ciudadella on Menorca, the harbour and marina at **Puerto de Alcúdia** is surrounded by restaurants and apartment blocks. The resort accommodation of this port reflects a variety of Spanish and Catalan architectural styles and these, in turn, are reflected in the waters of this vast bay — Bahia de Alcúdia. Puerto de Alcúdia has the longest beach of all Mallorca's seventy-five listed beaches which runs right around in a great sweep to Ca'n Picafort. The three beaches here really run into each other — Aucanada, to the north of the port, and Platja D'Alcudia continuing east to Platja de Muro. Offshore from the marina is the tiny islet of Aucanada with its little lighthouse.

The best souvenirs to look out for in Puerto de Alcúdia are the basketwork, hats, mats etc made out of woven palm leaves, a speciality of this region. The route now runs south-east out of Puerto Alcudia, alongside the beaches towards Ca'n Picafort. All along this area there are residential developments like Ciudads Blanca, Los Lagos and Gaviota. The road leads around the bay but, inland, to the right, is the great marshy region known as La Albufera.

La Albufera simply means the lagoon, or the salt lake by the sea. Almost a replica of Lake Albufera in the north of Menorca, it lies inland from the magnificent sweep of Alcudia Bay's beaches and is a great attraction for ornithologists. As with the Albufera on Menorca, this area of marshy sedges and reed beds, has a large lake, Esperanza, and these swampy regions attract more than two hundred species of resident and migrant birdlife. Before visiting this reserve one should apply to the offices in the Playa Esperanza Urbanisation in Alcúdia. La Albufera was once a large rice cultivation area and, around the middle of the nineteenth century, an interprising Englishman drained much of the water so that more agricultural land could be utilised.

Once a fishing hamlet, **Ca'n Picafort** is now a popular resort in the centre of the bay. Apart from its attraction as a bayside beach, there are several Phoenician remains in the form of a necropolis which stands on an islet, the Isla d'en Porros, near Son Real, between the road, which runs inland from the coast at this point, and the sea. Son Real is the site of prehistoric *talayot* remains. Although the road follows the line of the Bahia de Alcúdia, it cuts inland around the higher coastal land eventually meeting with the road to Isla Ravena and Colonia de San Pedro (or Sant Pere) and continuing into the town of Artá.

Eastern Mallorca

The eastern part of Mallorca includes the range of mountains known as the Sierra de Levante and an indented coastline concealing some of the most attractive and popular beaches and bays in the Balearic Islands. From Cabo Ferrutx, in the north, to Cabo de Salines in the far south, almost thirty of the island's seventy-five listed beaches offer holidaymakers a wide range of coastal resorts to choose from and several spectacular caves and prehistoric or Moorish ruins to explore.

The region's twelve main towns — including the island's third largest, Manacor, with 27,000 population, and the famous medieval town of Artá — offers the visitor the diversity of historic sites and traditional markets; while the Artá, or Levante, range of mountains, provides numerous opportunities for country strolls and visits to see some of the island's more important cottage industries.

This route commences in the far eastern point of Mallorca and covers the region around the ancient town of Artá, continuing down the east coast and its numerous resorts and sites of interest, to the southernmost point of the island. From here the tour continues to include the region around the south-east of Mallorca to end within striking distance of Palma de Mallorca itself. At times the main route hugs the indented coastline and occasionally detours inland, so that smaller side roads or tracks must be used to reach the little bays and secluded beaches of this popular coast. However, there are many boat trips to several of the more important resorts and beaches. Southwards from Cala Ratjada to the resort of Cala Santanyi there are around a dozen locations from which regular boat excursions can be made. These include Cala Ratajada itself, Cala Canyamel, Cala Millor, Porto Cristo beach, Cala d'or, Porto Petro, Cala Figuera and several others. This is by far the most pleasant way of seeing this coast and its varied attractions.

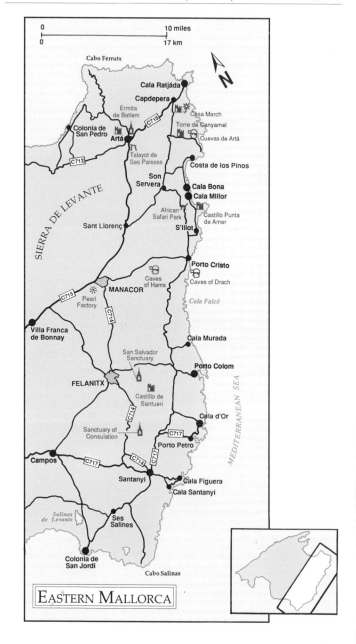

EASTERN MALLORCA

The fortifications and sanctuary on Puig Sant Salvador in Artá

There is a wonderful view of Artá and its church from the Sant Salvador fortifications

The best place to start a tour of a few days along the eastern coastline of the island is the hilltop town of **Artá**. It is a town of great antiquity, being known as *Jartan* by the Moors, but it is even older and was possibly founded by Phoenician traders. Dominating the region, the vast medieval church and fortress on the hilltop is an impressive sight and other points of interest in this picturesque old town are the sixteenth-century parish church, a seventeenth-century convent (San Fransisco), and the *almudayna*, or town hall. The Artá Museum in the Plaza de Ayuntamiento has displays of prehistory, exhibits from the Roman era and a tableaux called the Martes Balearicos showing the development of Mallorca and its people through history. The town itself is ringed with the remains of historic fortifications and a popular tourist attraction is the weekly market on a Tuesday morning.

Just to the north of the town centre is the mount, or Puig Sant Salvador which boasts a fortified church and early medieval castle. First constructed by the Moors the tower, or Torre San Miguel, and its ramparts may date even earlier. On the south side of Artá town is the famous site of Talayot des Ses Paisses. Built sometime between the seventh and second centuries BC the main hall of this prehistoric village comprises of a number of columns with a dramatic entranceway. The *talayot* of Ses Paisses is a typical Bronze Age structure and has an interior corridor. Some of the great blocks of stone used in the construction of this prehistoric village weigh around eight tons each.

Colonia de San Pedro is a small hamlet easily reached north-west of Artá; nearby is the *talayotic* archaeological site of Son Real. Not far away, but only reached by a road from Artá, is the ancient hermitage known as the Ermità de Betlem with a panoramic view of the Bahia de Alcúdia. To one side of San Pedro and north of the hermitage is the peak of Atalaya de Morey and Cabo Ferrutx, a headland on the tip of the eastern flank of Mallorca. Inland from this coastal route is the site of the Sa Canova Bronze Age *talayot* megalith.

Towards the east coastline is another ancient citadel, that of **Capdepera**. Just a short distance north-west of the town itself is the impressive Castillo de Capdepera built on a small hill. Constructed in 1300 the battlements of this castellated fort were completed eighty-six years later. Inside the fort are a chapel of 1316, the Moorish Torre d'en Nuis bastion and the governor's house from early eighteenth century. Capdepera itself is a fortified town with more than 400m of castellated walls, four defence towers and an impressive entrance. In the walls King Sancho constructed a tiny sanctuary, the

Oratory of Our Lady of Good Hope. King Jaime I, in 1232, used Capdepera as a base from which to lure the Moors on Menorca into serfdom. The town itself is full of historic houses and a weekly market is held in the town every Wednesday morning.

Located on the road to the coast from Capdepera town is another site of tourist interest, the gardens of Casa March, a landscaped area around a particularly spectacular villa. Known locally as the 'Sa Torre Cega', this building is almost a palace although it was built in 1911. The range of sculptures by famous artists displayed on the lawns and in the gardens is stunning because of their rarity and diversity. Out on the coastline, with its cliffs, coves and sandy bays is the headland of the Faro de Cap Depera (Capdepera lighthouse), and the little cape of Farayo.

Taking the road south from Capdepera, or a minor road east from the town of Artá, one of the most spectacular structures in this north-east region is the Torre de Canyamel. This castellated fortress overlooks the valley outside Costa de Los Pinos and the point, or headland. Often known as the Tower of the Montso, this square fort has three encircling defensive walls and contains a small museum of early Mallorcan tools. The tower itself dates from both Moorish and medieval times. The tower overlooks and guards its own little beach, the Playa de Canyamel.

The most famous beach in the Capdepera municipality is that which lies north of the Casa March, out on a small peninsula, the Cala Ratjada. Other resort beaches of this picturesque landscape include Son Moll, Cala Lliteras, Cala Mesquida, Cala Gat, Cala Agulla and Sa Font de Sa Cala.

From these beaches one must go inland to meet the road which runs down to one of the area's most spectacular sites.

The **Cuevas de Artá** lie around 9½km (6 miles) from Artá town on the coastline cliffs of the Vermell headland, and are a series of natural caverns hollowed out from the soft limestone rock. It is known that in 1230 over a thousand Moors hid here until King Jaime smoked them out, and Jules Verne got the idea for his novel *Journey to the Centre of the Earth* from visiting the cave system. Steps take visiting parties down a sheer cliff face, through an enormous cave entrance into great halls with stalagtites and stalagmites of different colours and hues. Some caverns are the size of a cathedral, while elsewhere the limestone formations meet to form great pillars and bastions. One 22m (72ft) high column is known as the 'Queen' another set of columns resembles a series of organ pipes. The many weird shapes and awe-inspiring size of the caves and their formations has led to

Torre de Canyamel is typical of fortresses throughout the Balearic Islands

Mallorca's east coast has many delightful ports like Porto Colom

this grotto, together with the Drach Caves and the Hams Caverns further south along the coast, to be regarded as two of the most important cavern system of their kind anywhere.

The **Cabo de Pinar**, or Cape of Pines, shelters more bays as the road continues south. Here are several comparatively new resort areas like the Costa de los Pinos, which is also named after the many pine trees in this region. The beach here is of a fine white sand. Further on, Port Vey and Port Nou are both quiet and have their own secluded bays and beaches.

From here Son Servera town is located a short way inland and not often visited, except on Friday mornings when there is a local market in the town. Back on the coast are more resorts and secluded bays. **Cala Bona**, for example, was once an old fishing village and port, but now has several new artificial beaches.

Another significant tourist area here is the bay of **Cala Millor** with a large, flat, sandy beach which is safe for children. Sports facilities include the golf course at Punta Rotja-Port Vell, fifty tennis courts and all the usual sea and sand activities and entertainments of a well-developed resort area.

Rounding the beaches of Cala Millor it is possible to view, to the left, the Castillo Punta de Amer, on the headland of the same name. Just beyond here is the Sa Coma complex. Sa Coma has a long beach and is a new development from which one can make excursions to the castle with its nearby African Safari Park, which is a drive-through open zoo, and the *talayot* prehistoric remains at Na Pol. The next small bay is Cala Moreya, but within easy reach is the small beach of the resort of **S'Illot.** Popular with Mallorcans, this tiny hamlet celebrates its 'Virgin of August' festival on the fifteenth of that month. Moving on to the next well-known bay, a side road cuts down from the main route to many small bays, among which is the notable Cala Morlanda.

Porto Cristo is the next large town on the route and this lies inland from the main line of the coast up a deep inlet. An ancient sleepy fishing village, Porto Cristo's first excitement came during the Spanish Civil War when Republican forces numbering 12,000 men took the port in 1936. This was the only action ever seen on Mallorca during the war and the occupation only lasted for a few weeks. Since early in the nineteenth century Porto Cristo has been unable to avoid its popularity for the twin natural phenomonen which are located nearby: the Caves of Drach and the Caves of Hams.

The Drach Caves (Caves of the Dragons) is one of the major tourist attractions on this part of the coast. Similar in size and content to the

Artá Caves, stalagtites hang down from high arching caverns to meet with giant pillared stalagmites thrusting up from the cave's floor. A great lake fills one cavern and lighting effects reflect the spectacular limestone formations in its sparkingly clear water. Tunnels and bridges take the visitors around a system of caves, one of which is below sea level and is known as the 'Amphitheatre' which can seat up to 3,000 people. Torchlit musical concerts from shallow boats are performed daily on the waters of the Martel Lake in this cave. Lake Martel, named after its French discoverer, claims to be the largest underground lake in the world. Other chambers in these caverns are known as The Black Cave, The White Cave, The Frenchman's Cave and Archduke Louis Salvador's Cave. Other spectacles include formations known rather imaginatively as Diana's Baths, the Theatre of the Fairies and the Monk and Cactus. The 'Hall of Flags' chamber is particularly spectacular being 40m (130ft) high.

 Just off the road from Porto Cristo to Manacor on a hillside above the port are the Caves of Hams. Discovered in 1905, the Cuevas de Hams or Llams, with its famous Venice Sea, is smaller than the systems of Artá and of Drach. Its name 'Llams' is supposed to come from some of the stalagtites which hang like fish-hooks from the arched cave roof. Here there are seven main caverns known as Angel's Dream, the Cathedral, the Crib, the Enchanted Villa, the Madonna de Montserrat and Paradise Lost.

Keeping to the road that runs parallel to the coast, Porto Cristo has its own little bay and beach, the Playa Tropicana at Porto Cristo, and further south are the coves of Aguilar, the bay of Mendia and the famous Cala Falcó. It is inland from Cala Falco that another of Mallorca's 200 cave systems is located. These are the lesser-known Cuevas del Pirata, or Pirates' Caves. So many tiny bays indent this coast that it is not practical to name them all, but they include those of Vacas, Mangraner, Barquetas, Bota, Domingo and Cala Murada. There is a long stretch of inaccessible coast before the beach and bay of Cala Algar which is the first of the Porto Colom bays and resorts to be reached from the north.

Porto Colom is only a tiny-harboured fishing port, but, because inland is the overshadowing town of Felanitx, it has become the centre of the seaside resorts here. Puerto Colom is another place which claims to be the birthplace of Christopher Columbus. From here it is well worth an excursion to Felanitx and its surrounding monuments. Inland from Porto Colom is the San Salvador Sanctuary of 1348, built as a castle and still in use as a hermitage. Several fifteenth-century artifacts in the sanctuary are well worth seeing, like the altar piece and the statue of the Virgin. There is a dramatic monument to Christ the King on Mount Picot. About 3km due south of the sanctuary but only found by taking a narrow track from near Felanitx are the ruins of the impressive Castillo de Santueri. This Moorish fortress is thought to be one of the oldest castles on Mallorca and is said to date from Roman times. It is one of the three main Royal castles built on the island, which include those of Pollença and Alaro. The foundations of the present castle were laid by King Jaime II, and in 1459 Charles of Naverre was held prisoner here.

The road maintains its distance from the rocky east coast as it heads through S'Horta, Calonge and Alqueria Blanca, and side roads lead down from the main route and these small towns to beaches and bays such as Cala Marcal, Cala d'Or, Cala Arsenau, Cala Ferrera, Cala Mitjana, Calaa Esmeralda, Cala Gran, Cala Llonga and the lagoon or lake of **Cala d'Or**. Main roads lead off the Santanyi road to Cala d'Or and its neighbouring fishing village of Porto Petro.

It is necessary to head inland to the town of **Santanyí** to reach the famous beach and bays of Cala Figuera. Santanyi itself boasts an ancient gateway, the Porta Murada, which has defended the small town for many centuries. This ancient monument, in Plaza Puerto, was built in the sixteenth century and was once part of the town's ramparts. In Plaza Mayor is the late fourteenth-century church of El Roser whose brickwork dates from Roman times and has been redesigned in Gothic style. The triple-arched bell tower is of interest as is its Rococco organ.

North-west of Alqueria Blanca is the Sanctario de la Consolacio, or Sanctuary of Consulation, which originally was built in the fifteenth century but has been added to many times. A feature of the sanctuary is the beautiful statue of the Virgin in the main building.

Porto Petro, or Peter's Port, is a picturesque fishing village now popular with the yachting fraternity. A small river sometimes runs into the deep inlet nearby. Several small bays such as Cala Mondrago can be visited near here. However, by far the main attraction on this part of the coast is **Cala Figuera**, a resort with all the attributes of cliffs, pine groves and watersport facilities. There is a good harbour in this traditional fishing village, known as the Venice of Mallorca and regarded by many as the island's most beautiful seaside town, while many tiny bays are within easy striking distance. Further south are the two lovely bays of Cala Santanyí and Cala Llombards. Between these two is 'Es Pontas', a good example of a sea arch, cut through a protruding cliff and bridging turquoise waters.

Although several more bays further south attract visitors for their seclusion, most travellers will rejoin the road which leads through Santanyí to the town of Ses Salines in the Botanicactus region. The name indicates that the scenery has changed to a drier, sandy and salty climate which encourages the growth of cactus and scrub. Between Santanyi and **Ses Salinas** is a small side road which leads to Cabo de Ses Salinas, the most southerly headland on the island from where one can look across the 17km (10 miles) of the narrow strait to the seventeen islands and islets which make up the Cabrera archipelago.

In the Ses Salines region there are several prehistoric ruins, such as the Sa Taliaia Joana village and the *talayotic* remains at Na Mera, Es Mitja Gran and Es Antigors. As the name implies, this region was famous for its salt probably before Phoenecian times, but it was these Middle-Eastern traders which left evidence of their visits on the Isla de Na Guardia. Several Roman escapades off the southern point left galley wrecks around these shores. More modern remains lie scattered around this area like the S'Estany tower near the great salt flats of the Salinas de Levante. This was built in the fifteenth century as a fort to guard the salt shipments, but the watchtower of the C'en Barbara and that on the S'Avall estates near the parish church, were probably built a century later.

There is not much to see in this rather bleak, desert area unless one is an ornothologist, botanist or archaeologist. Nor is there much of interest in the village of Ses Salines apart from the town's market, held every Thursday morning. There is a ferry to Palma from the nearby coastal port of **Colonia de Sant Jordi,** where a market is held every Wednesday morning.

From Colonia de Sant Jordi the road heads inland to the town of Campos, although there are still more bays and coves to the west of the port, especially the long white beach of Es Trenc where access is gained at **Ses Covetes.** There are kilometres of unspoilt sand and dunes untouched by tourism. However, by the time one goes very far around the headlands to the west, the countryside becomes more deserted and wild and the bays become less frequent. If one wants to take the more coastal route it is possible, but the roads are not good and there is little to see. On the road from Colonia de Sant Jordi to Campos the oratory of Sal Blas is worth a visit. The church in **Campos** has two important fifteenth-century paintings, the *Sa Mare de Deu de la Llet* and the *Bon Jesus de la Palencia*. On Calle Convento, the church of Minimos has an architecturally interesting façade dating from the seventeenth century. Of the four town defence towers still in existence the two best preserved are those in Calle Santanyi and the one

Fishing is still an important occupation for many Mallorcans

Many roadside verges, as here near Manacor, are covered with springtime flowers

on the Plaza Major in the town centre. Most visitors take the inland road from Campos which leads via Llucmajor to Palma de Mallorca.

The major town on this eastern part of Mallorca is **Mānacor**, which is now the island of Mallorca's second largest town — although the region of Calvia, in the south-west, claims it has the largest conurbation because of tourist hotel and apartment developments. Calvia claims a population of 37,000, followed by Manacor (27,000) and Inca (21,000). However, Manacor is a town of great importance for its simulated pearl industry. The world-famous manufacturing company, Majorica, is the main employer in this eastern township and the factory attracts many thousands of tourist visitors each year. The making of 'Perlas de Manacor' can be seen in the showrooms in the town's main church square,. and, although they are no cheaper than elsewhere on Mallorca, the choice is larger The other major industries are those of pottery and cabinet-making. Earthenware pots and fired roof tiles also make good souvenirs and most of Mallorca's furniture is made in the Manacor workshops. This is also a busy market town and fairs are regularly hosted here. The main market is held every Monday morning.

Manacor was founded by King Jaime II in the thirteenth century. Although built on the site of an ancient Moorish settlement and near the Roman site of *Cunium*, there are few sites of archaeological and historic interest in Manacor. However, the convent of Santo Domingo has an unusually tall bell tower which resembles a minaret, and a beautiful twin-storied seventeenth-century cloister. The remains of the ancient Torre de Palau stand near the marketplace. Little is now left of this *alcazar*, or royal palace, but a better preserved monument can be seen nearby. This is a medieval tower, the Torre de Ses Puntas, which has an interesting style of Gothic window and now houses a small archaeological museum with a display of ancient coins unearthed in the vicinity.

Just outside the town is the basilica of Son Pereto, an ancient Roman civic building which was converted into a Christisan church in the fifth century. One of only two triple-naved basilicas which have survived in Mallorca, the other being at Sa Corrotja in Porto Cristo. Mosaics and artifacts of historic and religious significance have been found in and around the basilica and are now on display in the museum of the Torre de Ses Puntas.

Market browsing, shopping, or watching the local craftspeople creating the typical dark, earthenware pottery or firing pearls with a secret ingredient, are the main attractions for the visitor, although Manacor now has a horse-trotting race track.

Mallorca's Central Plain and Southern Coast

Between the twin, parallel ranges of mountains, the Sierra de Tramontana and the Sierra de Levante, lies a large, flat area to the north-east of Palma de Mallorca and stretching as far as the wide bay of Alcudia. Midway between the capital and the northern coast lies Mallorca's fourth largest town, the industrial centre of Inca, population 21,000, well known for its Thursday morning market and its shoe industry.

Agricultural activities dominate the flat scenery which is punctuated by ageing windmills, little whitewashed farmsteads with ochre-coloured tiled roofs, and small woods and orchards which divide the patchwork of cultivation. Most of the towns are situated on the few small hills which break the monotonous plain and twelve of these towns have brown up from those founded by King Jaime III from around 1300AD onwards. Three main highways cross the plain from Palma and here the central region is described by following these routes. Describing almost a straight line, and running parallel to the Sierra de Tramontana range of mountains, the island's most frequented road runs from Palma, through Santa Maria and Inca, to Alcúdia and Pollença in the north-east; running directly east another route links Palma, Manacor and Porto Cristo in the middle of the island's east coast, eventually leading to the towns of Artá and Capdepera in the north-east. A third highway runs south-east from Palma to Campos Del Puerto, Santanyi and Porto Petro in the far south of Mallorca.

PALMA TO POLLENCA

Currently a freeway is being constructed to link the popular north coast with Palma city, as the weight of traffic on the secondary route which runs through several ancient towns is affecting the lives of the inhabitants and some of the older buildings along its route. However, if one is in no hurry and wishes to visit the old and picturesque locations in the centre of the island, the route through Santa Maria and Inca should be taken.

The secondary road, the C713, to Pollença from Palma centre follows the Palma to Inca railway and, once the city outskirts have been cleared, the satellite township of Rafal and the village of Pont d'Inca which holds its market day on Fridays have been passed, the road runs straight towards Santa Maria town.

However, before one reaches this town, at the turning off right to **La Cabañeta**, is the turretted manor of Son Veri with a display of paintings, ceramics, brocades and local treasures; it may be visited only by application in writing. A little further along the road is **Santa Maria,** an ancient town of some importance. The Convent of Minimos in Santa Maria is one of the village's most outstanding structures, as is the sixteenth-century convent dedicated to Santa Maria de la Real. This one of the village's oldest buildings and its small museum houses an exhibition of artifacts from the house of Conrado. The church nearby contains a fifteenth-century painting of the Madonna and boy child. In the ancient Minimos walls is a *bodega*, or grocery store, where the region's fine red wines can be sampled. The village has a market every Sunday morning, where local produce such as almonds can be bought.

From Santa Maria it is possible to take a diversion off the Inca road to visit the little, steep-streeted, sleepy village of **Alaró**. On Friday afternoons the village comes alive with its weekly market. Most tours to this village, with its majestically situated ruined castle, turn off at the town of Consell, so there are two alternative routes. Castillo de Alaró is about 3km (2 miles) past the village on a rocky outcrop reminiscent of a film set. The castle dates from the thirteenth century when the island's heroes Brassa and Cabrit defended this stronghold against Alfonso of Aragon late that century. There is a seventeenth-century hermitage built inside the castle ruins with some fascinating murals and an altarstone with carvings telling the tale of the two heroes.

Back on the Inca road the next township is **Consell**. A cottage industry has grown up here in the making of the straw shoes known as *alpargetas*, but there is little more to be said for the little town which does not even have its own market as it is overshadowed by the much larger town of Binissalem a little way to the north.

Binissalem once belonged to an Arab named Salem and was founded later by King Jaime II in 1300. The parish church of San Jaime, which originally dates from 1364, has been renovated several times in the last 600 years. Here some excellent marblework now decorates the interior while its exterior sports an octagonal dome and tower. Binissalem's weekly market falls on a Friday morning and the village can get very busy with traders from the surrounding countryside. This little town is famed for the quality of its red wine and also for the strange fox-like dog, the Ca'de Bou, which also comes from this region. One famous attraction is the Casa Sureda, a typical Mallorcan country villa open to the public. Just near the centre of the town, on the Palma to Inca road, is the waxwork museum of the Mallorcan theatre, the Museo de Cera.

The most influential town on the road from Palma to the north

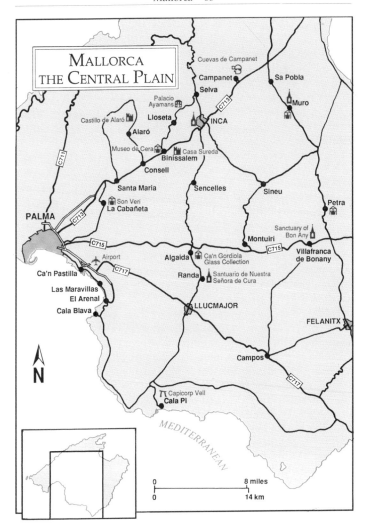

MALLORCA
THE CENTRAL PLAIN

Cuevas de Campanet
Campanet
Selva
Sa Pobla
Palacio
Ayamans
Lloseta
Muro
Castillo de Alaró
INCA
Alaró
C711
C713
Museo de Cera
Casa Sureda
Binissalem
Consell
Santa Maria
Sencelles
Sineu
Son Veri
Petra
La Cabañeta
PALMA
C715
Sanctuary of
Bon Any
Montuiri
Airport
C715
Villafranca
de Bonany
Ca'n Pastilla
Algaida
Ca'n Gordiola
Glass Collection
C717
Randa
Santuario de Nuestra
Señora de Cura
Las Maravillas
El Arenal
Cala Blava
LLUCMAJOR
FELANITX

N

Campos

Capicorp Vell
Cala Pi

C717

MEDITERRANEAN

0   8 miles
0   14 km

coastal resorts is **Inca**. Located in the centre of the plains, Inca is almost halfway between the capital and Pollença. This was once a Moorish stronghold and a Muslim mosque once stood on the site of the San Bartolome convent. Once a significant industrial centre and wine making area, Inca now specialises in producing shoes, leather goods and textiles for the local and tourist trade. The region around

Inca is also an agricultural centre and November sees its local farmer's fair. The railway from Palma northwards now terminates at the tiny station in Inca; it formerly continued through Manacor to Artá. Inca is Mallorca's third most important town, and its centre is dominated by the Gothic-cum-Baroque church of Santa Maria la Major. The bell tower is notable and the Renaissance altar is overlooked by a gold-framed Madonna which has been dated to the year 1373. Other ancient monuments include the convent of Santo Domingo and the convent of San Fransisco.

There are several good restaurants in Inca and one in particular, the Ca'n Amer Cellars, is well-known for being built into the old wine cellars — it is almost a small museum with ancient presses and artifacts from the vintner's trade decorating the walls. Another well-known eating house is the Inn of Son Fuster which serves traditional Inca delicacies including the special cakes called *concos d'Inca* made originally at the convent of San Jeronimo, and its piquant sucking pit roasted in herbs. Inca's market is a popular tourist attraction and many visitors flock to the town on Thursday mornings to shop for leather goods (which are often cheaper than at home or elsewhere on Mallorca) and souvenirs.

Heading out of the town a road to the east rises up to the Puig d'Inca and the monastery and sanctuary of Santa Magdelena. From the summit of the Puig d'Inca the distant Bay of Pollença can be seen. The views from here are dramatic and the agricultural importance of the area is immediately evident by the patchwork of fields and the many windmills dotted across the plains.

A short diversion west from Inca, on a side road which doubles back in the same direction as the Palma to Inca railway, is the village of **Lloseta** to visit the Palacio Ayamans — one of the grand country villas of the March family — which contains grand furnishings and antiques. The Madonna in the thirteenth-century church of Lloseta was, according to legend, discovered by a shepherd who was drawn to its hiding place by a shining light. It is said that the usually veiled statue has disappeared from the church three times since it was adopted by the church. To the north-west of Inca is the little town of **Selva**. The thirteenth-century church, whose interior has been rebuilt since a fire in 1855, has an ancient decorated façade and a long, cypress-lined stairway leading up to it, similar to that in Pollença.

About halfway between Inca and the Bahia de Alcúdia there are several important sites which can be visited. A side road to the right of the C713 route takes the visitor past many windmills, via Sa Pobla (La Puebla), with its spired church, to the town of **Muro**. Muro has a spectacular Gothic-style church, built in 1570, which has the largest nave interior of any church on the island, being 46m (150ft) by 16m (52ft) and 25m (82ft) high. The church's bell tower, once a watch turret, is 46m (150ft) in height. The convent of Minimos, and St Ann's church next door, built in 1560, has impressive cloisters where once dog fights and bullfights were held. The stone of this region is pure white and the Muro bullring is also built of the same stone. It was completed in 1910 and seats 6,000 spectators. In two ancient buildings on Mayor 15 are the exhibits of the Ethnological Museum including many ancient tools from the surrounding countryside which is famed for its basketwork, woven hats and rug making. The town of Muro holds its weekly market on Sunday mornings.

Doubling back through little Sa Pobla, whose market is held on a Sunday morning, to the main road, the next site of interest lies on the left side of the highway. The Cuevas de Campanet were discovered just about 50 years ago, and the road leading to the caves is almost opposite the spot where the Sa Pobla road meets the C713. The ancient church of San Miguel is located near to the entrance of the limestone grotto. The formation of stalagtites and stalagmites known as the 'Enchanted Town' is particularly enthralling.

Returning to the main road from Campanet and its caverns, the traveller can either branch left to the large town of Pollença and its satellite resort of Puerto Pollença, or continue north to the ancient town of Alcúdia and the resort of Puerto Alcúdia.

PALMA TO PORTO CRISTO

This route cuts diagonally across Mallorca from Palma in the south-west to Manacor, the second largest town on the island and then to the north-east coast. The road runs across the wide, open, central agricultural plain dotted with windmills and *fincas* or farmhouses, and over the eastern range of hills. Leaving Palma one should take the C715 towards Manacor from the eastern side of the city. This runs north of the airport eastwards, past the open-air Prehistoric Park — where along the roadside there are reproductions in stone of prehistoric creatures — to a crossroads. Just to the south is **Algaida**, a quiet, agricultural town with two market days, one on Tuesday morning and the other on Sunday morning. To the north is the famous exhibition of glassware called the Ca'n Gordiola Collection. Housed in a sort of castle, the glassworks known as the Vidreries Siglo XVIII celebrates the history of glass glowing made by the same family since 1719. There are exhibitions and glass blowing workshops.

*Inca's market attracts
visitors from many of
the tourist resorts*

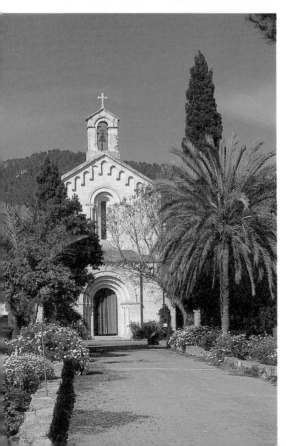

*A roadside church
at Crestatx, north of
Sa Pobla*

While in this area you could drive through Algaida to the little town of Randa and the monastery of Nuestra Senora de Cura, which is described in the Palma to Porto Colom route.

The C715 road now runs east through more agricultural land to **Montuiri**, just off to the left. The area is remarkable for the great numbers of windmills to be seen. There is also an ancient ruined convent here. Montuiri's market is held on Monday mornings.

Further north is the large town of **Sineu**. This was once the Moorish town of *Sixneu* and in the thirteenth century King Jaime II constructed a large palace here which is now the convent of the Immaculada. In the fourteenth century King Sancho declared Sineu to be the centre of Mallorca. The parish church here was converted from an old Arab mosque. On Wednesday mornings the local market is held in the town and you can buy the strong drink *aguardiente* which is made locally from cane. The largest tourist attraction in the town is the S'Estacio Art Gallery open from Tuesdays to Sundays.

By taking the Inca road west out of Sineu it is possible to take a turning towards Sencelles, to visit the Iberio-Balearic Fauna Museum at the tiny ancient village of **Costitx**. The market here is held on Saturday mornings. Further on the C715 road runs through **Villa Franca de Bonany**. North of the town, but only reached by a road from Petra, is the sanctuary of Bon Any. A vast statue of Christ surmounts the dome and its treasures include two triptych and an ancient Madonna.

Just a short distance north of Villa Franca de Bonany is the town of **Petra**, still retaining its Arabic name which means 'rock'. Petra is the birthplace of Fray Junipero Serra, the founder of California. The friar was born in Petra in 1713, about 60 years after a plague had decimated the town's population, and he died and is buried in Monterry, California in 1784. The Junipero Serra Museum and the manor house of the same name are well worth visiting and they now belong to the City of San Fransisco. The church of San Pedro (1582) here has some interesting artifacts from Junipero Serra's time and the monastery of San Bernadino (1672) nearby is also worth visiting.

From Petra one can take the north road to the coast on the Bay of Alcúdia, or return back to the C715 and continue east to Manacor and then north to the famous town of Artá or east to the coast at Porto Cristo.

PALMA TO PORTO COLOM

The main harbour boulevard from the centre of Palma heads out east with fine views across the bay and of the city itself. This is the

Autopista de Levant, the eastern highway which runs out past the garden city and its picturesque windmills known as Ciudad Jardi, with a turning to the left to the Son Sant Juan international airport — the busiest holiday airport in Europe. Continuing south-east along the boulevard the road passes the resorts of **Cala Gamba**, **Cala Esancia** and **Ca'n Pastilla**. This region is known as the Platja de Palma and its nine beach facilities continue along a spectacular stretch of sand past Las Maravillas, to the **El Arenal** resort area. The beaches along this eastern arm of the Bay of Palma are said to be among the best in the world and the thousands of holidaymakers to be seen on these beautiful white sands underlines their popularity, as does the high rise accommodation which inevitably accompanies these throngs. Just after the El Arenal beach the signpost indicates Llucmajor, a turning off to the left, away from the coast.

One point of interest in the Playa de Palma region, apart from the sunbathing, windsurfing, dinghy sailing and beachside entertainments is the La Porciuncula, on Calle Padre Bartolome Salva. This curiously named church has interesting displays of ceramics, ancient coins and archaeological artifacts in its museum. Set on a rise about halfway between C'an Pastilla and El Arenal, this Fransiscan church is open to the public daily apart from service times.

If, instead of taking the Llucmajor turning, one continued south along the coast the road almost terminates at the famous beach resort area of **Cala Blava**, and, a little further on, is the headland of Cabo Enderrocat. However, on the route to **Llucmajor**, the road climbs slowly up to the plateau on which the town is located. The main plaza of Llucmajor is dominated by its town hall which was built in 1882, and sports a fine bell tower. History has made its mark on the town as is seen in its mixed architectural styles. The town's two weekly markets are held on Wednesday and Sunday mornings and a popular treat to buy here is a sample of one of the local jams or preserves.

One of the main attractions in this region is the prehistoric site of Capicorp Vell. This is to be found far to the south of Llucmajor and is signposted off the road to Cala Pi on the southern coast. Dating from about 1200BC this prehistoric site consists of the outlines of twenty-eight dwellings overshadowed by five *talayots*.The Archduke Ludwig Salvador excavated this site in 1920 and Capicorp Vell is now an important national monument. Artifacts from this archaeological site are now on display in the Archaeological Museum in Barcelona.

To the north of Lluccmajor and near Randa is the spectacular Santuario de Nuestra Señora de Cura, perched high on the peak of

Puig de Randa. On the way up to the Fransiscan monastery one passes the Oratory of Nuestra Señora de Gracia, where there is a small restaurant, and the Oratory of San Honorato. Reaching the hermitage at the summit of the conical mount, the museum here contains many of the works of Llull. It is in this sanctuary that the great scholar and island hero, Ramon Llull, in the latter part of the thirteenth century, wrote much of his acclaimed work on Arabic studies with the assistance of a Moorish slave. The view from the monastery, 546m (1,800ft) above sea level, is stunning and the pretty little village of Randa itself lies on the plain below the Puig de Randa.

Back in Lluchmajor the route to the east coast runs straight across the plain passing a stone cross marking the spot where King Jaime III was killed by Peter of Aragon's forces in 1349 while attempting to invade the island. The next town is **Campos**, built on an ancient Roman site. Inside the church of this tiny town is a painting, *Jesus de la Paciencia (Christ in Pilate's Hall)*, attributed to Murillo. There is little else to see in Campos, but its market is held on Thursday mornings.

Heading north-east now out of Campos the road cuts across plains to the agricultural town of **Felanitx**. It is an ancient town with prehistoric beginnings, which can be seen at Monta la Mola and nearby El Cerro de San Nicolas. The town also has Roman origins and there are several interesting monuments in the town and its vicinity. These include the former convent of San Augustin and the Spanish Baroque parish church.

The main places of interest in the area are the Santuario de San Salvador and Castillo de Santueri, which have already been described.

Additional Information

Places of Interest

Palma de Mallorca
Note that most of the other mansions and buildings (apart from churches) mentioned in the text but not listed here are not open to the public and only the exterior may be admired.

Archives of the Kingdom of Mallorca
Ramon Llull 3
☎ 725999
Open: 9am-2pm, 4-8pm. Sat 9am-1.30pm, closed Sun.

Arab Baths
Serra 3 (near seafront)
☎ 721549
Open: daily 10am-1.30pm, 4-6pm.

Ayuntamiento (old town hall)
Plaza Cort
Open:Mon to Fri 9.30am-1.30pm, 4-6.30pm, Sat 9.30am-1.30pm.

Bellas Artes (art exhibitions)
Unio 3
Open: 11am-1.30pm, 6-9pm.

Casa Oleo (mansion small museum)
Calle Almudaina
Open: 11am-1.30pm, 5-8pm.

Castillo de Bellver
West of city
☎ 230657
Open: Oct to Mar 8am-6pm, Apr to Sept 8am-8pm.

La Seo Cathedral
Plaza Almirante Moreno
Open: 10am-12.30pm, 4-6.30pm.
Sat 10am-2pm. Closed Sun and holidays.

Cathedral Museum
Palau Reial 29 (adjacent to
  Episcopal Palace)
☎ 723130
Open: 10am-12.30pm, 4-6.30pm, 10am-1.30pm.

La Lonja (fine arts gallery)
Paseo Sagrera (near port)
☎ 711705
Open only for exhibitions 11am-2pm, 5-9pm. Sun and festivals 11am-2pm, closed Mon.

Mallorca Museum
Portella 5 (near cathedral)
☎ 717540
Open: 10am-2pm, 4-7pm. Sun 10am-2pm. Closed Mon.

Mallorca Church Museum
Episcopal Palace
Mirador 7 (near cathedral)
☎ 714063
Open:Apr toOct10am-1.30pm,3-8pm.
Nov to Mar 10am-1.30pm, 3-6pm. Sat, Sun and festivals 10am-1.30pm.

Municipal Museum of History
Bellver Castle
☎ 230657
Open: Oct to Mar 8am-6pm, Apr to Sept 8am-8pm.

Museo Krekovic (art collection)
☎ 246662
Queretano Quarter (east of city)
Open: Mon to Sat 10am-1.15pm, 3-6pm.

Museum of National Heritage
Almudaina Palace
Palau Reial (near cathedral)
☎ 714368
Open: Apr to Sept 10am-2pm, 4-6.30pm. Oct to Mar 10.30am-2pm, 4-6pm. Closed later on Sat and closed Sun.

San Fransisco
Plaza San Fransisco (east of city
  centre)
☎ 712695
Open: 9.30am-1pm, 3.30-7pm.
Open Sun mornings.

San Miguel
San Miguel 2 (north-east of city
  centre)
☎ 715455
Open: Mon to Sat 8am-1pm, 5-8.15pm. Sun and festivals times vary.

Santa Eulalia
Plaza Santa Eulalia (city centre)
☎ 714625
Open: Mon to Fri 7am-1.30pm, 5-9pm. Sat 7am-1.30pm, 4-9pm. Sun and festivals open at 8am.

Santa Margarita
San Miguel 48
☎ 725658
Open Mon to Fri 9.30am-11am, 5.30-7pm Sat and Sun 9.30-11am, 5-7pm.

Santa Magdelena (Chapel Santa
  Catalina Thomas)
Plaza Santa Magdelena (just off La
  Rambla)
☎ 715154
Open: daily 6-8pm.

Peublo Español (Spanish village)
☎ 237075
Captain Mesquida Veny 39 (west of
  city)
Open: 9am-8pm. Shop: 10am-6pm.

Solleric Palace (art museum)
San Cayetano 10
☎ 722092
Open: 11am-1.30pm, 5-7.30pm. Sat
11am-1.30pm. Closed Sun and
Mon.

Alcúdia
Municipal Museum of Archaeology
Calle San Jaime 2
Open: 10.30am-1.30pm, 3.30-
6.30pm. Closed Mon.

Algaida
Ca'n Gordiola Glass Collection
Palma to Manacor road at km 19.
☎ 665046
Open: summer 9am-1.30pm, 3-
8pm, winter 9am-1pm, 3-7pm, Sun
9am-12noon.

Artá
Artá Museum
Rafael Blanes 8
☎ 562020
Prehistoric and Roman exhibition
with Mallorcan tableaux.
Open: 10am-12noon. Closed Sat
and Sun.

Banyalbufar
La Granja (stately country house)
☎ 610032
Open: daily summer 10am-7pm,
winter 9.30am-6pm.

Binissalem
Casa Sureda (Mallorcan villa)
St Vicente de Paul 8
☎ 512186
Open: 9.30am-7pm. Closed Sun
and holidays.

Museo de Cera (waxworks museum
  of Mallorcan theatre)
On Palma to Inca road at km 25
☎ 511228
Open: daily summer 9am-8pm,
winter 9am-7pm.

Palacio Ayamans (Mallorcan palace)
Selva near Lloseta
Open: summer only, Mon-Sat
10am-5pm.

La Cabañeta
Son Veri (Mallorcan palace museum)
Off Palma to Inca road
Admission only by application in
writing.

Capdepera
Casa March (landscaped villa
  gardens)
East of Capdepera
Visits by arrangement with local
Office of Information and Tourism.

Torre de Canyamel (fortress)
South of Capdepera
Key to tower available from
restaurant next door.

The Artá Caves
South-east of Arta, south of
  Capdepera.
☎ 563295
Open: summer 9.30am-7pm, winter
9.30am-5pm.

Castillo Punta de Amer (African
  Safari Park)
South of Cala Millor
☎ 585425
Open: mid-Apr to Oct 9am-7pm
daily.

Costa d'en Balnes
Dolphinarium
Resort and entertainment centre, with dolphins and seals.
Open: daily, summer 10.30am-12.30pm, 3-6.45pm. Winter 10.30am-12.30pm, 3-5pm.

Costitx
Iberio-Balearic Fauna Museum
Open: daily summer 9am-1pm, 6-9pm, winter 9.30am-1pm, 3-7pm.

Deia
Son Marroig Collection (artifacts from Archduke Salvador's collection)
On Carterra Valldemossa to Deia road
☎ 639158
Open: Summer 9.30am-2.30pm, 4.30-6pm daily. Winter 4.30-8pm, closed Sun.

Archaeological Museum
Open to public by request from the caretaker.

Genova
Genova Caves
West of Palma
☎ 402387
Open: 10am-1pm, 4-6pm daily.

Lluch
Sanctuary of the Virgin of Lluch
The Augustinian monastery and museum. Simple overnight accommodation available.
☎ 517025
Open: daily summer 10am-7pm, winter 10am-5pm.

Chapel of San Pedro
Escorca village
☎ 517025
Open: daily, summer 10am-7pm, winter 10am-5.30pm.

Llucmajor
Capicorp Vell (prehistoric village)
Near Cala Pi on south coast
☎ 661626
Open: 10am-6pm daily, except Thurs.

Santuario de Nuestra Senora de Cura (sanctuary, monastery and museum)
On Puig de Randa
Enquire locally for details.

Manacor
Majorica (factory and showrooms of the simulated pearl industry)
Near the market.
☎ 550200
Open: 9am-12.30pm, 3-7pm. Sat and Sun 10am-1pm.

Torre de Ses Puntas (tower with small archaeological museum)
Centre of town.
☎ 551902
Open: by arrangement with the curator, 10am-3pm.

Muro
Ethnological Museum
Mayor 15
☎ 717540
Open: 10am-2pm, 4-7pm; Sun 10am-2pm. Closed Mon.

Cuevas de Campanet (caves with 'Enchanted Town' formations)
Near Campanet
☎ 563295
Open: daily summer 9.30am-7pm, winter 10am-6pm.

Petra
Junipero Serra Museum and Casa Solariega (manor house)
Calle Junipero Serra
☎ 561028
Open: 9am-8pm daily.

Pollença
Municipal Museum
Convento de San Domingo
In town centre
☎ 530108
Open: Tues, Thurs and Sun 10am-12noon.

Porto Cristo
Caves of Drach
South of Porto Cristo
☎ 570020 and 570774
Open: Daily tours every hour, summer 10am-5pm, winter 11am-5pm. Concerts on Lake Martel except on 4pm and 5pm winter tours.

Mallorca Aquarium
Near Caves of Drach
☎ 490704
Open: Daily 9am-7pm.

Cuevas del Hams
West of Porto Cristo
☎ 570227
Open: 10am-1.20pm. Every 15min with concert.

Cuevas del Pirata
Behind Cala Falco.
Open: daily 10am-5pm.

Puerto Alcúdia
Hidropark
Avenida Tucan
☎ 547072
Open: daily from 10am.

Puerto de Pollença
Anglada Museum (paintings by the artist Anglanda Camarasa)
Paseo Anglada Camarasa 87
☎ 531149
Open: 4-7pm daily except Wed and festivals.

Santa Maria
Los Minimos Convent
Casa Conrado Collection
☎ 620174
Open: 4-7pm, closed Sun.

Santa Ponça
Aqua Park
On Cala Figuera to Magalluf road.
☎ 680811
Open: mid-Apr to Oct 10am-8pm daily.

Sineu
S'Estacio Art Gallery
☎ 520750
Open: Tues to Sat 11am-1pm, 5-8pm; Sun 11am-1pm, 5-7pm.

Soller
Raxa Jardines (country house and gardens)
To the west of the Soller to Palma road and railway
Open: daily 10am-5pm.

Alfabia Jardines (landscaped gardens)
On the east side of the Soller to Palma road.
☎ 613123
Open: Apr to Oct 9.30am-6.30pm, Nov to Mar 9.30am-5pm.

The Soller House of Culture
Calle del Mar 5
Open: 4-6pm. Closed Sun.

Valldemossa
Palacio del Rey Sancho
First palace of the Mallorcan kings.
☎ 612106
Open: Oct to Mar 9.30am-1pm, 3-5.30pm; open until 6.30pm the rest of the year. Concerts performed here regularly.

Real Cartuja (Carthusian monastery)
☎ 612106
Open: Oct to Mar 9.30am-1pm, 3-5.30pm; open until 6.30pm the rest of the year.
Mallorcan folk dance performances in square. Tickets give entry to both the palace, the monastery and the pharmacy museum.

House of Saint Catalina Thomas
Open: Oct to Mar 9.30am-1pm, 3-5pm. Closed Sun.

San Bruno Nunnery Museum
Open: Oct to Mar 9.30am-1pm, 3-5pm. Closed Sun.

Tourist Information Offices

Palma de Mallorca
The Tourist Board offices are located near the station on Plaza Espana, ☎ 711527, on Aveninda Jaime III, ☎ 712216 and 11 Santa Domingo, ☎ 724090.

Accommodation

Hotels for the independent traveller include:

Palma
5-star
Melia Victoria Sol ☎ 234342

4-star
Bellver-Sol ☎ 238008
Iberotel Uto Palace ☎ 401211
Melio Victoria ☎ 234342
Nixe Palace ☎ 403811
Palas Atenea-Sol ☎ 281400
Raquet Club ☎ 280050
Son Vida Sheraton ☎ 790000
Valparaiso Palace ☎ 400411

3-star
Costa Azul ☎ 231940
Drach ☎ 223146
Jaime III Sol ☎ 725943
Rembrant ☎ 400361
Saratoga ☎ 727240

Costa de los Pintos
4-star
Eurotel Golf Punta Rotja ☎ 567600

Felanitx
3-star
Cala Ferrara ☎ 657650

Formentor
5-star
Formentor ☎ 531300

Illetas
5-star
Melia de Mar ☎ 402511

Llucmayor
3-star
Maionis Palm Sol ☎ 266750

Paguera
4-star
Gran Hotel Sunna Park ☎ 686750
Villamil ☎ 686050

Youth Hostels
There are two youth hostels in the Balearic Islands, both on Mallorca. For full details of the hostels and membership see the *IYHF Guide to Budget Accommodation* vol 1.

Alcúdia
Ctra Cabo Pinar
☎ 543395

Palma de Mallorca
'Playa de Palma'
Calle Costa Brava
13 Ca'n Pastilla
☎ 260892

years later, leaving more than 200 of their strange megaliths as evidence of their culture to survive to this day. Within 400 years the Iron Age civilization had arrived in Menorca followed closely by the Phonecians and then the Greeks from the eastern Mediterranean.

Few traces remain of these latter two groups of settlers, except pottery sherds, a few statues and the vestiges of the name the Greeks gave the island — *Meloussa* or 'Isle of Cattle'. One of the earliest groups to settle on Menorca and set up trading posts on the island, the Phoenecians, called it *Nura*, or 'Isle of Fire'. The Romans gave the island the name of *Minorca* meaning the 'Little One' compared to *Majorca* the 'Large One'.

Cartheginian invaders, arriving on Menorca named Mahon the capital city after their General Magon (Hannibal's brother) and set up many shrines and temples to their favourite goddess, Tanit, in caves and on prominent points around the island. The Cartheginian influence transformed Menorca from about 520BC and this occupation existed on the island for nearly 400 years until the advent of the Roman General Quintus Cecilius Metullus in around 123BC.

The Roman Empire protected and nurtured the city and its large harbour, which they named *Portus Magonis*, for more than 550 years. The advantages of Mahon's sheltered harbour were invaluable to the empire's sea trade. The city then went through a period of occupation by Germanic Vandals in around 426AD, the Byzantines in 525AD and then the Arabs in about 902AD.

The Moors named the island *Minurka* and established their capital and religious centre at Ciudadella, naming it *Medina Minurka*. For 400 years the Moors ruled from Mahon until King Alphonso III of Aragon landed in the capital and ousted the Arabs in 1278. Christianity was subsequently restored and many Moorish mosques were torn down to make way for churches and convents, most of which were built with fortifications against the pirates which still frequented this part of the Mediterranean. The famous pirate Barbarossa sacked Mahon in 1535 and then the Turks, subjected the island's second city, Ciudadella, to the same treatment 23 years later.

Plague, smallpox and cholera ravaged the city up until the early seventeenth century and Philip II, in 1570, evacuated the island's surviving 5,000 inhabitants. In 1644 King Charles II of England negotiated with the Spanish for rights to use the harbour of Mahon for his trading vessels. Although the capital in name, and the island's largest town by the turn of the century, Mahon was still regarded as second to the then capital of Cuidadella. Mahon was not officially recognised as Menorca's capital until 1721. By the beginning of the eighteenth century the political climate again changed.

In 1708 the British began nearly a century of rule in Menorca transforming the city and erecting a great many grand buildings. Sir Richard Kane, who arrived to assume governorship of the island in 1712, created orchards around Mahon's harbour and is remembered in a monument at Es Vergers near the capital. Kane, who transferred the capital from Ciudadella to Mahon, and who died in 1736, also imported the Freisian cattle which are now a prominent sight on the island. A labyrinth of underground military passages were created under the capital during the war with the French in the mid-eighteenth century and the Duke de Richelieu, landing in the north west and crossing the island to the outskirts of Mahon, laid seige to the English-held city in 1756.

A fleet under the English Admiral Byng, sent to relieve the city, about turned and sailed to defend Gibraltar. This act resulted in the court-marshal and subsequent execution of Byng, and the loss of Menorca to the French. A period of French rule lasted seven years until 1763. In 1778 Mahon and the island came under Spanish rule and the city's first bishop was appointed by the Vatican in 1795.

After Nelson's defeat of the Napoleonic fleet Sir Charles Stuart took Mahon but his occupation only lasted until 1802 when the island was finally restored to the Spanish. The English left much evidence of their culture in Mahon and it is said that Nelson himself was a visitor to Golden Farm, a British-built villa on the northern shore of Mahon harbour, in 1799. A sudden decline in trade and prosperity hit Mahon during the mid-nineteenth century with the advent of steamships which did not need the shelter of the island's vast harbour. But the first inter-island ferry service commenced from Mahon in 1852, heralding the coming of the era of tourism.

The English left much evidence of their culture in Mahon, together with numerous buildings typical of the British style of the period. Classic Georgian architectural edifices remain testament to the number of wealthy Englishmen who resided in Mahon. Today the sash windows of these Mahon houses, the only ones to be found in Spain, are named *winderes*, a reminder of the English word used for them during the seventeenth and eighteenth centuries. The city's bow windows are still called *boinders* today and the grand side-boards found in many of Mahon's houses are called *saydbors*.

Today Menorca is one of the quieter islands as far as tourism is concerned, but that does not mean that all its beaches are uncrowded and tourists do not flood the popular markets. Around thirty main beach resorts are easily accessible around Menorca's shores and

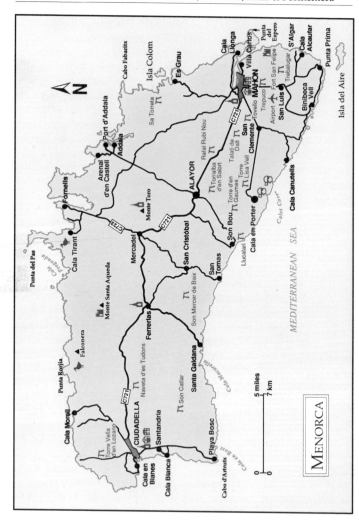

around forty other coves, bays and beaches await discovery around the island's rocky, indented coastline. Several excellent bird-watching regions dot the island's perimeter and the varied, undulating landscape inland offers many pretty walks and tours to Menorca's prehistoric sites and places of historic interest, including the grand *fincas*, or Menorcan country farmhouses.

Cool stone, elegant patios, fine staircases and open courtyards are typical features of the Menorcan villa

In Mahon there are many examples of English architectural styles

MENORCA'S BEACH RESORTS

San Tomas
Long, white sandy beach resort with hotels and apartments on the front and up into the pine covered slopes facing the beach.

Cala en Porter
Protected by cliffs this inlet narrows to a beach with golden sand reached by steps from the busy town. Shops, bars and restaurants edge the beach. The cliffside Cave of Xoroi has a bar and disco.

Son Bou
Menorca's longest beach with gently shelving fine lemon-coloured sand. This beach becomes less crowded further west from the ugly tourist hotels. Currents here can be dangerous at times but the beach offers a wide variety of watersports.

Cala Santa Galdana
A crescent of golden sand surrounded by pine-covered cliffs protecting clear, calm waters. Three large hotels do not enhance this bay's beauty. There is boat hire, mini golf, a windsurfing and a diving school. The beach is popular with families.

Cala en Bosc
Ringed by holiday villas a safe, pink-sanded beach on one side of the marina. Watersports facilities and a small bar on the beach.

Cala Blanca
Often crowded, this popular white sand beach has bars and restaurants. The waters are very safe; caves in the cliffs to explore.

Cala Morell
A rocky cove with a small beach of coarse sand. No watersports facilities although the shallow water is ideal for snorkelling.

Arenal de S'Olla
Near the Son Parc development, this expansive beach, edged with high dunes, has pinky sand and clear, shallow waters. Every sort of waterspor. Shop, restaurant and bar on the beach.

The main towns of Menorca are steeped in history and the island has close links with its English past. Four major markets attract the Menorquin locals as well as the visitor eager for leatherwork, handbags, shoes, jewellery, cheeses, earthenware items and pottery.

Arenal d'en Castell
This wide, circular bay is very popular and dramatic, only marred by clifftop hotels and apartments. There are five restaurant bars on the beach which shelves slightly, dropping off to deep water. Numerous beach facilities including sailboat and motorboat hire.

Cala Mesquida
Reddish sand fringes the deep waters of this cove A little castle on a promontory divides the beach. Popular at weekends.

Platja de Son Xoriguer
Twin beaches of white sand and clear water, both have bars and the larger has a restaurant and shops. All manner of watersports for hire, including parascending and ski-bob. Club Falco offers diving tuition.

Platja de Sant Adeodat
A narrow beach next to Sant Tomas, with no watersports facilities. The narrow golden-sanded beach has a small bar.

Cala de Binibeca
This tiny beach has the extraordinary Binibeca fishing village complex with its dazzling white apartments and curved walkways. Good sand, shallow water and a bar-restaurant make it very popular for families.

Platja de Punta Prima
Easily reached from Mahon, this wide, white sand beach has watersport hire and is near a shopping complex. There are bar-restaurants both off and on the shore, where water currents can sometimes be dangerous.

Cala d'Alcaufar
A sheltered, shallow cove with a fine, narrow beach reached through a picturesque row of typical fisherman's cottages. The bay is popular with boaters and fishermen and has a bar-restaurant and many sites to explore on its headlands. There is only one hotel behind the beach.

Folklore displays, craftwork exhibits and musical performances entertain visitors in the cultural centres and some hotels. Menorcan hotels and bars are, in general, not the brash establishments associated with some of Spain's mainland and other island resorts. Nor do discos and evening clubs cater for the package deal holiday-maker who has generally over-indulged in beer or wine. The Menorcan people pride themselves on providing a comparatively quite sedate location for those tourists and visitors who appreciate their island and the rowdy holiday-maker is firmly discouraged.

Up-to-date information useful to the visitor who intends to travel around Menorca can be found in the English language magazine for tourists *Roqueta*, or from local tourist board offices. Most hotel receptions stock useful details of car rental services, excursions, bus times, local activities and entertainments. From hunting and fishing to diving and horse riding, the island offers a wealth of diversions and caters for most sports such as golf, horse racing, tennis, sailing, or even cricket. Most visitors however, will want to explore the island's interior as well as search out the spectacular bays and beaches and Menorca is an ideal size for day excursions.

Menorca has a good network of roads, although few of them are surfaced. The basic structure of the island's highways and byeways is hinged around its main road which bisects Menorca from Mahon in the east to Ciudadella in the west. This is the C721 highway and routes to the north and south coast tend to be linked to this road, which also passes through the main towns of Alayor, Mercadel and Ferrerias. Most of Menorca's attractive bays, beaches and seaside resorts are accessible by road, although some may be little more than a cart track. Once the traffic congestion and the one-way systems of the two major towns has been overcome, driving on Menorca is easy and enjoyable. There are less than ten filling stations on the entire island and fuel is slightly cheaper than in many northern European countries. A good road map of Menorca is recommended for the explorer and there are a set of detailed military maps available on the island. There is no shortage of car hire companies on the island and taxi prices on the island are government controlled and therefore not expensive. A good, cheap bus service runs five times daily between Mahon and Ciudadella and many resort areas are served by the island's buses although it is best to check the frequency of the services. In Mahon the cross-island buses leave from Plaza de S'Esplanada and from Avenida Josep M. Quadrado. In Ciudadella buses depart from the top end of the Plaza de S'Esplanada. Bicycles can be rented at most major resorts and provide a good alternative to bus or car travel. A good book of suggested bicycle tours is produced in the local language and is available on Menorca.

ACCOMMODATION ON MENORCA

Most visitors to Menorca will either base themselves in one of the two major towns, in the smaller towns like San Luis, Alayor, Mercadel, Ferrerias or San Cristobal, or in one of the several leading resort regions which are dotted around Menorca's coastline like Villa Carlos, just outside Mahon, Binibeca, Cala en Porter, Son Bou, Arenal d'en Castell or Fornells. Apart from numerous rentals and apartments, the island has more than seventy listed hotels. These rate from four-star hotels like the Port Mahon Hotel in the old capital, the Audax in Ferrerias, or the Santo Tomas in San Cristobal, to the many single star hotels liberally distributed throughout the island.

Notable among Mahon's ten hotels is the three-star Capri and, for basic comfort the Hotel Noa, a two-star establishment, is not far from the town's centre. Villa Carlos, on the outskirts of Mahon has nine hotels, several of which stand out, like the Agamenon, the Rey Carlos III, The Hamilton, and the Sol del Este Mar, all three-star establishments. An attractive one-star hotel, Admiral Collingwood's former residence, the Hotel del Almirante, is historic and very popular.

Ciudadella, has more hotel accommodation than the other towns, three-star hotels including the Cala Blanca, the Club Falco, and the Calan Bosch. The Iberotel Almirante Farragut, is the most striking and largest of the town's three-star hotels.

Not far from Mahon, near the airport, the town of San Luis has several hotels including the three-star S'Algar and San Luis Hotel. South of San Luis is the striking tourist village of Binibeca Vell and, a little further west is the hippy resort of Cales Coves.

Right in the centre of the island of Menorca is Mercadel, a small town with seven hotels, two of which, both three-star rated, are named the Lord Nelson, one being residential appartments. Also almost in the centre of the island Alayor township has the Milanos Sol and the Pinguinos Sol, both three-star hotels.

Most independent visitors however, look for accommodation near the coastline and, at Fornells, on the north side, the Port Fornells hostel and Hotel S'Algaret, offer forty-three rooms between them. On the south coast, near the sea, is Cala en Porter, a tiny village with three hostels and two hotels including the one-star Acuarium.

Mahon

Mahon, or Mao as it is known in Menorcan Catalan Spanish, is the capital of Menorca and has a population of around 25,000. Unlike the capitals of its sister islands, Mahon lies a short distance inland and is reached from the ocean by a 3-mile long arm of the sea so deep that it is reminiscent of a Norwegian fjord. The sides of this flooded gorge are not as steep above the waterline as one would find in Norway, but they form the largest natural harbour in the Mediterranean and the second largest in the world after Pearl Harbor. Ferries run regularly from the port to Barcelona and Valencia, a sailing of approximately 10 hours, and there are also sailings to Palma de Mallorca.

There are steep cliffs on the south, or left side as one enters the port of Mahon, and low hills on its northern bank. Mahon's seaward entrance is guarded by a military installation on La Mola, part of the Punta del Espero; the Island of Lazare, or the Lazarete, once a quarantine centre but now a recuperation centre for the mainland's medical staff and a research station, lies to the right of the entrance. The earlier site of the quarantine hospital, used until 1817, was on the Isla Plana, or Flat Island, further out to sea.

The former need for quarantine facilities in Mahon was due to the importance of the large natural port, which once played host to ships from all over the world. To the left of the entrance stands the ruins of the ancient castle of San Felipe, known as Fort Marlborough when the island was in English hands. Rat Island which also lay in the channel, was blown up in the 1930s as it was a hazard to shipping.

The colour of the water, as Mahon is approached along this narrow inlet, is usually a brilliant ultramarine which reflects its depth and underlines the fact that this harbour is the second deepest natural port in the world. Passing to the left of the channel, known as Cala Sergo, one can see the spread of Villa Carlos.

From here one can look out across the channel to the magnificent Golden Farm, or Sant Antoni, where Admiral Lord Nelson and his consort, Lady Hamilton, are supposed to have stayed in 1799, and other splendid residences of the rich. The Isla de Rei, the Island of the King (named in 1287 after King Alphonso III landed there), with its church and naval buildings, lies almost in the centre of the channel and, on the north, or right bank, stands the eighteenth-century naval base station. Also on the north side of the inlet, opposite Villa Varlos (sometimes known as Es Castell) is the small settlement of Cala Llonga located almost midway along the promentory which forms the north shore of Mahon's deepwater channel. Few tourist visitors to Mahon today have the opportunity to see the capital from the sea as they will arrive by air.

It must be noted that street names and often place names both in Mahon and throughout the island, have changed perhaps more than once over the years and locals sometimes prefer the old placenames. It is not possible to explain all the name changes or list them here but a good up-to-date, large-scale map of Mahon can be obtained from the tourist office on the Plaza de la Constiticion.

An immediately striking feature of the town is what was once named Avenida de Victoria, now the Costa de Ses Voltes or Abundancia, which snakes up the steep hillside towards the church of Nuestra Señora del Carmen. Standing on Plaza del Carmen and much restored in the 1940s, the original church structure dates from 1751. Once a convent between 1726 and the early years of the nineteenth century, the Claustre del Carmen, just left of the church, is now a grocery market which trades in the famous local cheeses, fruit and vegetables. Mahon's main market is held throughout the year on Tuesday and Saturday mornings. The convent's huge cloisters now offer shade to the market traders.

To one side of the Plaza del Carmen is Plaza de España which leads down towards Plaza Reial, the famous American Bar and the English Library. The latter, on Costa d'en Deya, is a favorite meeting place for visitors. Behind the market, on Costa de Ses Voltes, is the local fish market while on the other side is the exhibition hall, which displays a map and document collection amassed by an island notary of the nineteenth century. The pedestrian shopping centre of Carrer Nou is down one of the two side streets leading off Plaza Reial.

From the wide avenue, Anden de Levante, which runs along the side of the harbour, pedestrians take the harbour steps to cut across the winding Costa de Ses Voltes. Visitors will note the large bust of Admiral Miranda on the stairway. This direction leads up past the church of Santa Maria to the town's main shopping area, Calle Dr Orfila. To one side, at the top of the town, is the popular meeting place of the Plaza de S'Esplanada and, to the other, the Parc des Freginal. Up out of Old Mahon is the great square of Plaza de S'Esplanada shaded by trees and bordered by eighteenth-century mansions and army barracks. The monument here is dedicated to those killed in the Spanish Civil War; there is a tourist board office in the square.

Walking up through the town several of the better preserved houses once lived in by eighteenth-century merchants and British Naval officers can be seen. The finest examples are on Calle Isabel II, Calle Dr Orfila and in the central parts of the city. Many of these houses contain fine and original examples of early English furniture, such as Sheraton and Chippendale pieces. Built by an Italian architect in 1824, the Teatro Principal, in Calle Deya, is now used as a cinema but it is Spain's oldest opera house. It is difficult to direct the visitor through the maze of narrow streets, alleyways and squares which comprise the outskirts of Mahon but the central area is well defined around the Plaza Espana, Plaza de la Conquista, the Plaza del Carmen and the market area.

High above the harbour as one docks at the ferry port, stands the massive bulk of the church of **Santa Maria de Mahon.** Founded in 1287 by King Alphonso III, its red roof contrasts with the white-painted houses which clamber up to it from the dockside. The city's fortress-like church has only one nave with a carved Baroque altar.

Mahon's quayside is a peaceful contrast to the busier harbours of Palma de Mallorca or Eivissa

An interesting visit can be made to the Xoriguer Gin Distillery in Mahon

Tree-lined boulevards in Mahon offer a tranquil environment for shopping and sight-seeing

Apart from its pierced bell tower Santa Maria's exterior seems plain but it contains a magnificent 1810 Baroque organ shipped from Barcelona, where it was made by a Swiss craftsman and then decorated by Mahon's own artists. This church organ has an amazing 3,006 pipes and four keyboards. Under the protection of Admiral Collingwood's fleet, the organ travelled to the island on the express wishes of the bishop of the city during the Napoleonic Wars. The church is now the centre of an annual international music festival.

 Over the road from the church of Santa Maria is the city's 1633 town hall, restored in 1788, and sporting its great London-made clock, a present from Governor Sir Richard Kane. An early stone-carved coat of arms of the city can be seen here together with a plaque commemorating Mahon's importance in the Empire of Rome. Plaza de Conquista, nearby, is fronted by a Georgian building housing the Casa de Cultura (now being restored and refurbished) once the Archaeological and Fine Arts Museum which has been moved to the cloisters and church of San Fransisco. Plaza de Conquista is the site of Mahon's ancient castle.

In the centre of the square stands a monument to King Alphonso III who ejected the Moors from the city in 1287. Calle San Roque leads from near the town hall, past the city's oldest monument, the ancient medieval gate, Puerta de San Roque, built in the reign of King Pedro IV of Aragon, on Plaza Bastion, to Calle Isabel II where several grand old palace buildings are located.

Along the Mahon waterfront among the larger, foreign yachts, are the unusual local fishing craft, with pointed prow and stern. Known as *llauds*, these boats are of ancient Arabic design and are still made to traditional specifications. From the Club Maritimo boat trips take visitors around the harbour. The houses along the waterfront each side of the docking area seem to be built into the cliffs and those with a red-brown colouring may have been painted with naval anti-fouling paint at the time of the British occupation.

 To the right of the commercial dock is the town's aquarium and the Xoriguer Gin Distillery where one can purchase a large variety of gins made in the shop's own distiller. Further on, towards the west of the town is the **Museo del Iglesia San Fransisco** where the Belle Artes collection and the exhibits of the Archaeological Museum are housed. A little alleyway around the corner from the eighteenth-century church of San Fransisco is named Es Pont d'es General and is said to be the only Moorish street in the city to survive to this day. In the opposite direction, the waterfront leads past many little bars and cafés down to the salubrious quarter of Cala Figuera with its exclusive moorings, boutiques, souvenir shops selling the local Lora pottery, and some exclusive restaurants. In and around Es Castell (Villa Carlos) further out of the city along the harbour inlet, there are more restaurants and nightspots and, on the quayside of Cala Fonts in Es Castell there are more bars, cafés and restaurants.

The deep, wide harbour inlet of Mahon divides the city from a long, narrow peninsula to the north. From the north-west of Mahon a road runs around the head of the sea inlet to the peninsula and the places of interest facing the city across the harbour. Much of this hilly promontory is set aside as a naval base and military zones but the road passes Golden Farm, or Predio de Sant Antoni. There are several attractive villas and farms in this region and the small settlement of **Cala Llonga** is located almost midway along the north shore of Mahon's deepwater channel.

Another pretty little cove on this side of the water is Cala Rata and, right at the end of the cliff-faced headland, stands La Mola, its fort situated more than 250ft above the sea. Around from La Mola is a high cliff called Cabo Negro which is not easy to get to except on sea excursions from Mahon which take visitors past this grand headland to the wide beach at **Cala Mezquida**. This resort area is popular with the inhabitants of Mahon as it is only a short drive from the capital, but there is little shade on the beach in summer. On the southern part of this large bay is the tiny islet of Sa Bateria Amagada. In the centre is an outcrop of rock surmounted by an old defence tower and, in the north of the bay, the great cliff of the Pa Gros headland stands out dark red against the blue of the sea.

Really a satellite town of Mahon, located on the southern side of the deep Mahon harbour, **Villa Carlos** is popular with many visitors to Menorca. Georgetown, as it was known to the British, was built initially as an army barracks with the city square, located by turning left on the Mahon road at a signpost for the town, constructed as the parade ground. The British Governor at the time, Sir John Mostyn, laid out the garrison's barracks in 1771 with what is now the spectacular Georgian town hall as its main building. Mostyn's troops had earlier taken the nearby Fort San Felipe, of which only a few tunnels remain. The Spanish demolished the main structure in the early nineteenth century, after re-possessing Es Castell and naming it Villa Carlos after King Charles III in 1782. Although it is nominally still a military zone visitors can obtain a pass to visit the military museum in the fortress.

There are several well-respected hotels in Villa Carlos and a popular place to find good restaurants is the fishing centre of Cala

Puerto de San Roque, Mahon's oldest monument

The broard sweep of Villa Carlos' promenade is lined with exciting cafés, bars and restaurants

Fonts to the south of the town on the harbourside. Sailing trips leave Cala Fonts for tours of Mahon harbour and nearby coves. Another cove which is popular with visitors to the town is Cala Corb which has several bars.

Ciudadella

Ciudadella, pronounced and spelt Ciutadella by the local people, is one of the Balearic Island's most historic settlements. It is certain that the Greeks, Phoenecians, Cartheginians and Romans were all aware that the island of Menorca had another fine harbour apart from that of Mahon in the east of the island. Ciudadella's port, located at the westernmost coast of the island, extends deep into the coast to form a natural harbour along a narrow inlet over a kilometre long. Easily defended the Phoenicians established a trading post here and, in about 400BC the Cartheginians subsequently founded a town around the inlet. In 902AD, after a number of raids extending over 200 years, the port was eventually adopted by the Moors after the Arab invasion of the island.

For four centuries the Moors established themselves in both Mahon and Ciudadella leaving numerous legacies of their architecture and culture which still survive to this day. The city has more of an Arabian look than its sister city of Mahon and the few remaining examples of Moorish building in Ciudadella are probably the last left on Menorca. Many of the Christian churches in the city have been constructed on the sites of earlier mosques. Parts of the city's town hall date back to the Moorish occupation of the eighth century. The Moors made Ciudadella a religious centre and their rule lasted until 1278 when King Alphonso III of Aragon landed on the island and ousted them. Alphonso immediately declared Ciudadella the island's official capital and transformed the great Arab mosque in the city into an impressive cathedral whose tower is probably a reconstructed minaret.

In the fourteenth-century a market was established in the city. The decimation of its population during the plagues almost led to a civil war between Mahon, the larger city, and Ciudadella, whose population had dwindled to several hundred by the mid-sixteenth century. It is said that the famous pirate Barbarossa, sacked Ciudadella some years after raiding Mahon in 1535 but, in 1558 the Turks, under General Mustapha, raided the city, destroyed all records, looted and sacked the find buildings and carried off many of the surviving population, which had expanded to several thousand, to sell in Constantinople as slaves. An obelisk in the centre of the city, the

Plaza d'es Born, commemorates this disaster.

In 1712, during the long British occupation of the island, the then Governor, Colonel Sir Richard Kane, linked the two cities of Mahon and Ciudadella by constructing a wide, straight road across the entire width of the island. Much of his road exists today. In 1722, Kane transferred the capital of Menorca from Ciudadella to Mahon. During the war between the British and French, a few years later in 1756, the Duke of Richelieu landed in Ciudadella and proceeded to Mahon where he laid seige to the British troops stationed there. Ciudadella's celebrated descendant, First Admiral of the US Navy, Admiral David Ferragut, son of an emigrant from the city, visited his father's birthplace in 1867 and was made honorary citizen.

From that time, apart from the Spanish Civil War, when the cathedral was ravaged, and two subsequent world wars, the city of Ciudadella slept peacefully in the backwaters of the Balearic Islands until the advent of the modern tourist trade. However, a link with its past as capital of the island remains, as Ciudadella is still the seat of the Roman Catholic bishop of the island, while many grand buildings also stand testament to the city's past glory.

After an eventful past Ciudadella is today a tranquil and attractive little 'city' of some 15,000 population. Grouped around the head of its picturesque harbour inlet, and spreading along its southern bank, many of the city's older buildings and places of interest are located around the grand, palm-shaped square known as the Plaza d'es Borne near the end of the port and the single tiny bridge which crosses Ciudadella harbour. The bridge leads onto Avenida Gabriel Roca on the harbour's north side where there is little of visitor interest except that the road leads eventually to some beautiful coves and beaches in the extreme west of the island.

Most travellers on the island approach Ciudadella through its eastern suburbs where there are several factories. One is a shoe factory started in the early nineteenth century by a native of the city after his manufacturing successes in Cuba. The first historic remains in the city which are seen on and near Calle General Sanjurjo, are the Portal de Sa Font, one of the city's original five gates, and parts of the ancient city walls which stood until the mid-eighteenth century. The Mahon Gate, as it is sometimes known, is not however, on the main road into Ciudadella, but is reached by taking the Calle Jose Antonio to the right on reaching the pretty Plaza Alphonso III. Here stands the Casa Vivo Esquella, an interesting example of local architecture. Calle Jose Antonio follows the old city wall and, taking a left turn at the Portal de Sa Font, several small roads lead into the pretty Ses

Voltes area of the city. Here are arcaded shops, shaded arched walkways and balconied houses of the French and English occupational periods. This part of Ciudadella, a maze of alleys and lanes, little restaurants and cafés, contains the Convent of Santa Clara to the right of which on Calle San Sebastian, is the Palace of Squella which contains a bed used by Napoleon. Admiral Ferragut stayed in this eighteenth-century family palace during his visit to the island in 1867. The staicase and elaborate wrought-iron balcony of the palace can be viewed from Carrer Sant Sebastia. The building is not open regularly but a guided tour can useually be arranged with the Tourist Information Office in the Borne. Just across the street is the **Episcopal Palace**, or Bishop's Palace, dating from the same era.

Next to the Bishop's Palace is Ciudadella's famous cathedral. This stands on the tiny square known as Plaza Pio XII. Once an Arab mosque stood on the site of the **Santa Maria cathedral** and the present building was completed in replacement of the Moslem structure by the year 1362, exactly 75 years after the Christians recaptured the island. The base of the cathedral's bell tower is all that remains of one of the minarets of the ancient Moorish mosque. The church, which is simple in its design as a result of being ransacked during the 1936 Spanish Civil war, was only consecrated as a cathedral in 1795 and points of interest include the altar canopy and fascinating stone carvings over the Puerta de la Luz doorway. Twelve Renaissance private chapels lead off the high, Catalan-style, main nave. Opposite the façade of the cathedral is the **Palacio Olivar** which houses an art and historical museum.

The church of del Rosario on Carrer Roser has an ornamental frontage carved in the beautifully coloured local stone and, cutting across the Plaza Pio XII, one comes to the **Palacio Torre Saura** on Carrer Santissima. This magnificent example of an early eighteenth-century noble's town house has been converted into an antique shop and has an impressive archway, decorative finials, a delightful courtyard and elegant staircase. The Palacio Martorell, a similar manor house, is located on the same street. The Palacio Salort, nearby, has a fine eighteenth-century interior. Some of these noble's houses can be visited by prior appointment with the family in residence through the city's tourist office.

The visitor is now in the centre of Ciudadella, in the Plaza d'es Born known locally as ' The Borne' or the 'palisades'. This attractive, palm tree lined plaza is flanked by some of the city's more important buildings such as the *ayuntamiento*, or town hall, which stands opposite the Torre Saura palace. The castellated tower of the town hall sports a clock and the interior contains many treasured paintings, Gothic decorations, a small museum and historic archives.

A number of other terracotta-coloured old buildings face the square. These are the gracious town houses of the eighteenth century, sharing space with cafés and bars. The church of San Fransisco stands on the south side of the Borne designed partly in Gothic and Baroque styles. In the centre of the Borne is a monument to those inhabitants who died defending Ciudadella during the invasion by the Turks in 1558. From the north of the Borne steps lead steeply

These colonnaded walkways are typical of Ciudadella's fascinating sidestreets

Napolean's bed in the Squella Palace, Ciudadella

On the 'Borne' are two of Ciudadella's many grandiose palaces, those of Saura and Salort

down to the city's little harbour and the sailing club can be reached by walking along the edge of the port's quayside past cafés and bars, some of which are set in the cliffside's natural caves. Back in the city centre, across Calle Cuesta, to the south-west corner of the Borne plaza, is the tree-dotted Plaza Colon, or Columbus Square, recently re-named Plaza de S'Esplanada. In the south-east corner of this plaza is the Avenida Negrete which leads onto the tiny city's ring road and the Avenida del Conquistador eventually linking with the Cami de Mao, or the Mahon road.

Eastern Menorca

The island is bisected laterally by the road which runs from the west (Ciudadella) to the east (Mahon), separating the northern, desert region of the island from the more arable south. However, as the airport is located in the east, and the island's capital and main port is in this region, many visitors to the island tend to congregate in the eastern part of the island. Accommodation for visitors is more concentrated in the east with hotels in the capital and in the smaller towns like San Luis, Bibibeca, Alayor, Mercadel, or San Cristóbal, or in one of the several leading resort regions which are dotted around Menorca's east coast like Villa Carlos just outside Mahon, Cala en Porter, Son Bou, Fornells or Arenal d'en Castell.

About half of Menorca's thirty main beaches and many of its places of interest are located in the east of the island. Prehistory left a wealth of megaliths and primitive settlements to explore and the island's highest peak, Monto Toro, at 357m (1,163ft), is located just east of the town of Mercadal. Several famous caves and stunning coastal cliffs are also to be found around the shores of the eastern half of the island. This half of Menorca offers numerous excursions to either its attractive beaches or, inland, to view the countryside, the little villages or larger agricultural or industrial townships.

Driving north of the capital, minor roads lead out to several well-known places on the coast between Mahon and Fornells. On the outskirts of Mahon is a statue to Governor Kane and then the flat market garden region known as Es Vergers. The first turning to the right off the PM710 road leads to the bird sanctuary and lake of S'Albufera and to the little fishing village of **Es Grau**.

The deserted housing complex of Sangri-La lies off to the left of this road. There is a large beach at Es Grau and, during the summer, one can take a boat trip out to Menorca's largest islet, the **Isla Colom** with its tentative connection with Christopher Columbus, or even an earlier pirate known as Colom who plundered shipping in the region. On the isle there are early Christian settlement ruins and ancient copper workings. The wild, rocky scenery here and numerous headlands offer fine views of the sea and Isla Colom.

Back on the Fornells road, the next turning to the right leads to the Cabo Favaritx and the attractive beach of Cala Presili. A little way along the road the remains can be seen of the road built to link Mahon with the west of the island in 1720 by the English Governor Kane, which branches to the left and Son Cardona complex to the right. Before the headland, tracks turning right off the main road after the church of Ermita de Fatima and the *faro* (lighthouse) signpost, lead to the important prehistoric Sa Torreta *talayot*. On reaching the cape and just before the lighthouse, several pretty beaches can be visited along the coastline to the south of the headland.

Returning again to the road to Fornells and a little further north a crossroads, just after the Binifabini complex on the right, leads either left to Alayor, or right to the little yacht haven of **Port d'Addaia**. A side road leads off to the popular resort beach of **Arenal d'en Castell** with its three hotels and apartment complex and to Na Macaret. The beach resort of Arenal de S'Olla, or Son Parc, is located just around the bay from Arenal d'en Castell, but must be approached by road along a separate turning off the Fornells road. A fork in this minor road leads along the peninsula to the Cueva Na Polica. This is a vast sea-cavern reached only from the ocean side which was discovered in 1831; it extends deep inland in a series of caves, lakes and tunnels.

If one continues north on the Mahon road the next crossroads indicate the large town of Mercadal to the left and the pleasant fishing village and great bay of **Fornells** to the right. In the village of Fornells is a seventeenth-century fortress and much of the outskirts around the harbour to the north and to the west of the headland has been devoted to large tourism developments. The Es Plau fish restaurant in Fornells has hosted many famous patrons including the King of Spain, Juan Carlos on one of his favourite sailing excursions.

A particular industry on which the village now thrives is sea bream farming. Tourism plays an important part in this region's economy — hotels, villas and apartment blocks are now part of the north-east's landscape. For watersports enthusiasts, the best areas are to be found out of the village, around either arm of the bay, where there are many shallow, sandy beaches as there is no real beach near to Fornells. The surrounding region is a favourite haunt of ornithologists as this part of the coast is the temporary home to a number of rare migratory birds.

Two roads lead south from Mahon. One runs directly south to the

A pretty Menorcan villa at Es Grau

Trepuco's prehistoric monuments are among the most famous in Europe

village of San Lluis and the other also leads to San Lluis but takes a roundabout diversion through the township of Es Castell (Villa Carlos). It is on the road running directly from Mahon to San Luis that more of the island's sights may be seen, particularly, along a turning to the right off the San Luis road, the prehistoric site of Trepuco. This is the location of an ancient settlement the tower of which, the *talayot*, is built of huge stones and surrounded by a wall built by the French in 1782 when they were attacking the English forces in nearby Fort San Felipe. The T-shaped *taula* is the largest prehistoric megalith on the island and both the *talayot* and *taula* can be seen from Mahon itself. There is a smaller, second *taula* and a large, circular precinct at this site which was occupied right up until the early sixteenth century. Trepuco, which dates from about 1,000BC, is one of at least 200 *talayot* sites on Menorca and contains two of the island's thirty *taulas*. It is probably the most visited of all Menorca's prehistoric monuments due to its proximity to Mahon.

Just past Spain's most easterly houses, the complex of Sol d'Este, is the military zone, army barracks and the ruins of Fort San Felipe on Punta de Sant Carlos. The fortress, which contains a military museum, is normally closed to visitors but passes may be obtained from the Guardia Civil in Villa Carlos. Fort San Felipe (Fort Marlborough to the English) may be reached by following the road south out of Villa Carlos to the little cove of Cala St Esteve, so named because the body of St Stephen, Christianity's first Martyr, was brought here en route to Spain in 417AD. The ruins of Marlborough's Fort, the Redoubt, built in the early years of the eighteenth century, stand on the cliff to one side of the bay and visitors can still explore its remaining tower, the Torre d'en Penjat. Stone from this fort was used by the Spanish to build the Lazaret in 1807.

Back on the main road from Villa Carlos to San Lluis, the pretty village of Trebaluger is reached and from here one can visit another prehistoric *talayot* site. Most of the archaeological sites are sign-posted from main roads and generally reached by well-worn tracks.

From Trebaluger the road enters the bright, whitewashed town of **San Luis**. A bye-pass now skirts the town which was built by the French in the eighteenth century and named after King Louis XV by its founder, the Duke of Richelieu. Today the town boasts a modern supermarket designed with the souvenir hunter in mind. The town's main market takes place every Monday and Wednesday mornings. St Lluis' most interesting sites include the 1761 Church of St Louis with the French Royal coat-of-arms emblazoned on its façade. The square on which the church stands sports a small fountain and an obelisk to the island's first French Governor, the Comte de Lannion. The striking windmill, Mola de Dalt, opposite the Placa Nova houses an interesting agricultural museum reflecting the importance of farming in this area during the French occupation of Menorca. San Lluis has a racetrack, an aeroclub and a football stadium and is the 'gateway' to the coast and tourist resorts of south-east Menorca.

The most popular of the rocky bays and beaches of the south-east coast include **Cala d'Alcaufar** with its hotels, villas and the **S'Algar** resort complex. S'Algar is easy to reach by bus or taxi from Mahon's Esplanada and a short walk takes the visitor to a scenic headland called Rinco des Rafelet, a geological spectacle. A little furthjer around the coast, also accessible from the city by bus, is **Cala Punta Prima** which faces the tiny islet known as Isla del Aire. Punta Prima cove is overlooked by the Torre de Ganxo, an ancient defensive watchtower on a headland just east of the bay.

Following the coastal road past wild, rocky scenery one can either divert to the village of Torret, or continue on to the famous Binibeca coastline. This little area comprises the pretty 'fishing village' of **Binibeca Vell**, an award-winning, modern, Moorish-style villa complex; the Binibeca Nou development; and the four beaches of Bibibeca, Binissafulla, Biniparratx and Binidali. The tiny islands offshore are known as Ilot de Binibeca and Ilot de Binissafulla. Only Binidali has any historic monument of significance, a large wall built several hundred years ago to protect the villagers from pirate raids. From Binidali the road runs inland towards the airport and San Clemente market village. However, first take the fork off to the left, which, although a cul-de-sac, leads down to Cala Canutells. This brand new resort has a small sandy beach surrounded by cliffs.

Some of Menoca's most impressive archaeological sites can be visited easily from **San Clemente**. The first, Torello, on the Mahon road, is the fifth-century Christian basilica ruin of Es Fornas de Torello with some beautiful mosaics. A little further along the road, just before the San Lluis Airport turn-off, is one of the largest *talayots* on the island and also a smaller *talayot* and settlement where several important ancient artifacts have been unearthed. Continuing back towards the capital, after the airport turning, can be seen the two *talayots* of Curnia, to the left of the road.

In order to reach the interesting coastline which runs along the south coast to San Tomas from the headlands of Es Canutells, back-track to San Clemente village and take the left fork to Cala En Porter.

The first feature to visit on this part of the coast is the famous Cales Coves where more than a hundred prehistoric burial caves, dating from the ninth to the seventh centuries BC, can be seen in the cliffside. One large cave here, known as Des Jurats, contains interesting inscriptions in Latin, while other caves further up the cliff slope date from the fourth century BC to about 350AD. The apartment complex of **Cala en Porter** can be reached by returning to the main road and turning down to the resort set on a hillside. The main feature here is the Cova D'en Xoroi, a natural cave where, according to legend Xoroi, or 'One Ear' the Barbary pirate, held an abducted local girl for many years until his whereabouts was revealed by footprints in the snow leading to his apprehension and suicidal death. The cave, with its balcony overhanging the sea far below, is now a bar and disco. Cala En Porter itself, a large and lively resort with many facilities, lies at the head of an inlet of the sea where its white sandy beach is generally packed with sun-worshippers.

One should return to the main road to reach the next bay, Cala Llucalari, the fishing hamlet of San Lorenzo, and the **Son Bou** resort development. The Platages de Son Bou, a favourite with people from the inland town of Alayor, make up the longest stretch of sandy beach and white dunes in the whole of Menorca. Here the hotels, apartments and a campsite of modern construction contrast with the prehistoric caves on Cap de Ses Penyes and the *talayot* settlement of Llucalari. At the cliff base are the ruins of an early Christian basilica and a fourth-century village known as Ses Canessies, discovered in 1851. Further west of the Son Bou resort, on low hills, stands the conurbation resort of San Jaime and then a wide area of marsh which is a haven for birdlife. This salty marshland lies between Son Bou and the coastal town of **San Tomas**, a pretty spot with attractive villas and a wide and popular beach.

A main highway bisects the island of Menorca from Mahon to Ciudadella and this is the road to take in order to view the sights at the centre of the island. Along this route, in the eastern part of Menorca, there are two major towns, Alayor, the island's third largest town, and Mercadel. However, branching off this road, and making tours from these towns the visitor can divert to see some of the island's archaeological sites and beauty spots. The first important prehistoric site reached along the Alayor road is to be found off to the left after the airport turn-off. This is known as the Talati de Dalt which sports the largest *taula* structure on the island. Building ruins, caves and a *talayot* comprise this ancient site and other minor sites in the area include the megaliths of Montple, the wells of Alcaidua and the twin *navetas*, or burial constructions, of the Rafal Rubi Nou site. Continuing along the main highway, almost to the town of Alayor

As well as modern hotels accommodation is also in traditionally-styled appartments like these at Binibeca Vell

Binibeca Vell, with its unusual apartments and fine beach, is one of the most popular resorts on Menorca

itself, a road leads off to the left, towards the seaside resort of Cala en Porter. Along this secondary road is the large site of Torralba d'en Salort, which is the most northerly of all the *talayot* settlement sites in the Balearic Islands. Terracotta heads of Tanit the Phoenecian fertility goddess and a bronze image of a bull have been recovered from the area, which dates back to around 1,000BC.

Further along this road, towards Cala en Porter, is another prehistoric location, the walled and arched *talayot* site of the Torre Llisa Vell. A third, and by far more impressive find in this part of the island, the So Na Cacana site, lies just a little further south of the Torre Llisa Vell *talayot*. With several building remains, two *taula* courtyards and two huge *talayots*, this place is thought to have been of great religious importance to the prehistoric inhabitants.

The largest prehistoric settlement site, the Torre d'en Guames, is found to the right of the Son Bou road just past the town of Alayor. Several housing ruins, two huge *talayots* and a *taula* make up the Gaumes site where a bronze helmet has been discovered and also an image of Imhotep the Egyptian priest and architect of the pyramids. Just a short distance south of Guames is the sepulchre site of Ses Roques Llises. Vast stone blocks have been erected here in the shape of a house with a rounded hole and passageway forming an entrance. This is a most unusual prehistoric construction.

Alayor, an industrial town based on the shoe making and cheese and ice cream producing industries, emerged from a farmstead established on the site in 1304. The streets are narrow, but fortunately the main road bypasses the centre. Several ancient building in Alayor include the church of Santa Eulalia, built between 1674 and 1680, which has an interestingly decorated interior with statues and carvings. The cloisters of the church of San Diego, called Sa Lluna are well worth a visit but, apart from purchasing a pair of local shoes, a sample of special cheese or an ice cream from the La Menorquina factory, there is little more to see in this agricultural township.

The last town of any size here, and almost in the centre of Menorca, is **Mercadel**. As one nears the town the great bulk of Monte Toro (Bull Mountain) dominates the landscape and, just before the road enters the town, the sandstone geological curiousity on the left side is known as Sa Penya Cabeza del Indio, or Indian Head Peak. The town of Mercadel stands on the crossing of two main roads which run north to south and east to west across Menorca. The shoe and biscuit industries are prevelant in Mercadel and now souvenirs such as earthenware pots and hats, supplement the local's income. The town has a good school and famous college and is well-known for its

Menorcan bars, cafés and good restaurants, one of which, the Moli d'es Reco, is in a large windmill.

Only two buildings of any significance are to be found in the town: the parish church of Sant Martin where the agricultural influence is indicated by the farm implements hung around the saint's statue, and the town hall. A famed son of Mercadel was Father Pedro Camps, who founded the town of St Augustine in Florida in 1768.

Monte Toro is 357m (1,171ft) high and a legend relates that its name came from a wild bull which, instead of attacking a group of monks on the mountain, led them to a cave where they discovered a statue of the Virgin and Child. Perched on the summit of Monte Toro, is the church of Our Lady of Toro next to the Santuario de Nuestra Senora de Toro, the church's convent. Today the Madonna statue in the church stands with a bull at her feet. A large statue of Christ with outstretched arms stands on a high point of the mountain, but the radar and TV masts tend to distract from the medieval atmosphere of the isolated mountain top.

Western Menorca

Drawing a line halfway across the island from Fornells on the north coast to Santo Tomas on the southern shores, the west of Menorca is a little more physically interesting than the eastern half. Two major geological features, La Vall, in the north-west, and the gorge of the Barranco d'Algendar, running into the island from the south coast, give this part of the country a more rugged appearance. In the west of the island prehistoric man erected a number of strange megaliths which are now tourist attractions, while the city of Ciudadella offers a wide selection of interesting places worth visiting.

The western part of Menorca has its fair share of popular beaches and coves and there are many spectacular cliffs and sea caves. Mount Falconera is located on the north-west coast and rises to 205m (672ft).

Cuidadella, the second largest town on the island, in the far west, has at least twenty hotels of varying star ratings and there are several other tourists resorts in this part of the island. These include Ferrerias, an important town in the centre of the west part of Menorca, Cala Santa Galdana on the south coast, and Cala Morell on western Menorca's north coast.

One of the less frequented excursions from Mercadel is to take the road north, keeping to the west of the salt marshes of Casa Nova, a good bird-watching region, to the rugged coastline of Punta del Pas. This road runs parallel to the one on the Fornells point. On the right is the large Cala Ferragut and the Fornells peninsula. On the eastern side of the long, narrow Punta del Pas is a popular resort for people from Mercadel, the *playas* or beaches of Cala Tirant, and on the west side is the beach of Sanitja. Arriving at the rugged tip of the Pas headland one can see the tiny Isla d'es Porros to the west. This spot is the most northerly point in the whole of the Balearic Islands.

The solitude of the rocky Cabo de Cabelleria and its isolated lighthouse contrasts with the unspoiled white sandy beaches of Binimel-La to the west of the Pas peninsula.

A little further west are the renown beaches of Cala Pregonda, Cala en Calderer and Cala del Pilar sand-strewn beach coves, one of which, Pregonda, has a small river which floods occasionally. The landscape and the coastline between Pregona and the mountain of Falconera, a short distance along the shore, is deserted and wild and the beaches beyond the 205m (672ft) peak of Falconera, are best reached by the roads which run to the coast from Ciudadella town.

To the southwest of Falconera's peak are the woods and farms of a low-lying area of particular beauty. Named La Vall, this is also a wildlife preserve and an important region for birdwatchers.

Just a short, but winding track inland from Cala Pregonda is an important historic monument, a Roman fortress which saw occupation by the Moors until 1287 against Alphonso III of Aragon when it fell into Spanish hands. This ancient citadel, once Menorca's major stronghold, stands on Monte Sant Agueda (200m, 656ft). It is a good hour's climb to reach the summit and the remains of the fortress, but the view from here is spectacular. From this hilltop ruin an ancient, paved walkway, partly obscured, leads south past the farm of Santa Cecilia, to the island's main road near the town of Ferrerias.

Ferrerias stands in the shadow of S'Enclusa, Menorca's second highest hill standing just 275m (902ft) high. This important fourteenth century town's name probably derives from its early reputation of making iron door hinges as *ferreria* is Catalan for a blacksmith. Ancient houses still stand to one side of the main Plaza Espanya and the town seems full of shops and children. Today Ferrerias specialises in furniture manufacture and producing a popular local dish which includes partridge. The neat, whitewashed church of Ermita San Bartolomeu, on Plaza de l'Esglesia in the town centre, has an elaborate early nineteenth-century interior.

One interesting detour to the south-east from Ferrerias leads to the pretty little village of **San Cristóbal** and to the beaches of Santo Tomás and San Aldeolato on the south coast. By diverting to the right of the San Cristóbal road one can visit the ancient site of Son Mercer de Baix. This prehistoric village, set high above the Son Fideu gorge,

Son Bou has Menorca's longest beach and is the site of an ancient Christian basilica

The rocky north coast has several secret bays like this one at Cala Morell

has an underground cave dwelling and a *naveta*, or burial house. Back on the Santo Tomas road the village of Es Migjorn Gran, or, more popularly, San Cristóbal, is an overspill of Ferrerias and was founded in the eighteenth century.

Another southerly route from Ferrerias takes the visitor through some attractive, green, agricultural landscape to the beach resort of **Santa Galdana**. This road follows one of the island's major physical features, the Barranco d'Algendar, a gorge-like valley containing a small river. The cove and beautiful sandy beach of Santa Galdana has been dubbed 'The Queen of Coves' as it is one of the most exquisite beaches on the island. Surrounded by a dramatic semi-circle of pine-clad rocks and with a small river refreshing its placid, turquoise water, this bay now has its quota of hotels, villas and apartments but, due to its position on the island's south coast, far from both Menorca's two major towns, it has not yet become too overcrowded.

A number of sandy coves and pretty bays are clustered along this part of the coast but most can only be reached by road from Ciudadella. The easiest way to see most of these bays and beaches is by boat. Many beaches have hire-boats which can be used to hop from cove to cove, taking in those on this south-west coast in an afternoon from Cala Galdana. **Marcarella** beach lies a short distance from the inlet of Galdana and this cove is linked by road to Ciudadella. So also is the next beach west along this rocky shoreline, the **Cala en Turqueta** with its low scrubby headlands and dazzling white soft-sanded beach. The road from Ciudadella passes, at the junction with the Macarella road, the site of San Juan de Missa. The tiny, lonely, eighteenth-century chapel is locked except on the feast day when the saint's followers make a pilgrimage from Ciudadells.

A series of cliffs jutting out into the sea divides Turqueta from Cala des Talaier, a totally secluded cove surrounded by pines and with a small, sheltered beach. For pure white sand on twin beaches in a pine-clad horseshoe bay one must choose the idyllic cove of the Playa de Son Saura. This secluded and remote cove can be reached by road and track through the Son Saura estate from Ciudadella. This road passes the prehistoric site of Son Catlar with its *talayots* and *taulas* and the remains of a small settlement.

Few roads or tracks link the three other beaches in this corner of Menorca with the island's second largest town but one road leads from Ciudadella down the west coast to the **Cabo d'Artrutx** which is the island's most south-westerly extreme and sports a lighthouse on its headland. From here one can take a trek across country past the Tamarinda farmhouse to the beach, marina, hotel and bayside village of **Cala en Bosc**, an increasingly popular sailing resort offering excursions around this part of the coast to other beaches such as the nearby popular twin resorts of Platja de Son Xoriguer. Just south of the town of Ciudadella, along the island's west coast is one of Menorca's oldest resort beaches at **Santandria**. Surrounded by bars and villas and fortified by an ancient watchtower, this inlet was apparently popular even in 1756 when the French Duke Richelieu landed here. Today, both this bay and **Cala Blanca**, a little further south, are both swarming with sailboards and windsurfers rather than the French frigates of yesteryear.

Within a small radius north of Ciudadella there are a number of places of interest and not least being the three deep inlets with little sandy beaches which lie to the west of the town. These are reached by taking the bridge across the head of the port turning left onto the Paseo de la Colonia (Avenida Gabriel Roca), which runs along the north side of Ciudadella harbour. These three beaches, Cala en Blanes, Cala en Brut, and the Los Delfinos resort at Cala 'n Forcat, are popular with the townspeople. The road terminates at Forcat and the coastline to the north of the headland is wild and rocky.

Taking the main north route out of Ciudadella, passing the Forcat road on the left, about halfway to the coast is the prehistoric site of the Torre Vella d'en Lozano which has several *talayots* and a ruined chamber. Continuing to the north coast one comes to the rocky hollow of Cala Pous and the steep, bleak cliffs of Cala Morts. Neither coves have a beach but offer spectacular seascape views. Nearby is the lighthouse headland of the Torre Nati.

If one returns to the north route as it leaves Ciudadella another branch takes the visitor north-east of the city, past the distinctive ancient watchtower of the Torre d'en Quart farm, skirting the pretty farming landscape of La Vall and heading northwards to the peak of Falconera. A turning to the left leads to the coast at the well-known **Cala Morell**. Prehistoric tombs and traces of ancient habitation dot this area and its beach is the only accessible one in this region.

Back on the road towards Mount Falconera, keeping La Vall on the right, the road more or less peters out at the sweeping sandy beach of Cala de Algairens sheltered to the east by **Punta Rotja**.

To the south of the Morell to Algairens road one cannot miss the upturned boat-shape of what is said to be Europe's oldest building. This is the Naveta d'es Tudons. In a remarkable state of preservation for its 3,000 years, around a hundred skeletons were discovered in this fascinating burial house which is just one of forty-five similar *navetas* to be found on Menorca.

Additional Information

Places of Interest

The majority of the places which attract visitors, apart from Menorca's beaches, are its prehistoric sites. Almost all sites are located off the main roads, in fields or in wild countryside and open to view.

In Mahon and Ciudadella there are several museums and historic buildings, churches or places of importance which have opening times which tend to vary between summer and winter.

Ciudadella

Episcal Palace
Early Bishop's Palace
Calle Bispo.
Open: Mon to Fri, 10am-1pm.

Santa Maria Cathedral
Fourteenth-century cathedral.
Plaza Pio X111
Open: 9.30am-1.30pm, 5-7pm.

Town Hall (museum, archives etc)
Plaza d'es Borne
Open: 8.30am-2.30pm.
Eighteenth-century town house.
Calle Bispo.

Interesting eighteenth-century noble's houses include:
Palacio Olivar (art and historical museum), Palacio Torre Saura (now an antique shop) and Palacio Martorell, Carrer Santissima, Squella Palace and Palacio Salort.
Open: summer 10am-2pm
Requests for entry must be made to the private families via the tourist office on the Borne
☎ 381050.

Mahon/Mao

Aquarium (Moll de Ponent)
Near waterfront
☎ 350537
Open: Winter from 8.30pm.
Summer open all day.

Casa de Cultura de Sa Nostra
S'Arravaleta, Dalt y Baix
31 Sant Jordi
Open: 6-9pm.

English Library
Ist Floor, Costa d'en Deya 2
☎ 362701
Open: Mon to Sat 10am-1pm.
Closed fiesta days.

Exhibition Hall (map and document collection)
Near town centre
Open: 8.30am-2.30pm.

Fort San Felipe and Military Museum
South of harbour entrance near Villa Carlos
Passes from Guardia Civil in Villa Carlos
Open: Sat-Sun, 11am-1pm.

Library/Museum
On Plaza de la Conquista
Open: 10am-2pm, 4.30-9pm. Closed Sun and Mon.

Museo del Ateneo (marine specimens and map archive)
25 Sa Rovellada de Dalt
Open: 6.30-9pm.

Museo del Iglesia San Fransisco (fine arts and archaeology)
West of town centre
Open: 10am-1.30pm, 4-7pm.

Museum
Conte de Cifuentes 25
☎ 360553
Open: 10am-2pm, 4-10pm.

Naveta d'es Tudons, one of the most visited prehistoric sites on Menorca

The magnificent inlet of Cala Santa Galdana, 'Queen of Coves'

Teatro Principal de Mao (early 19th-century theatre and opera house) 46 Calle Costa d'en Deia.

Xoriguer Gin Distillery
Near waterfront
☎ 362192
Open: 8am-7pm.

San Luis
Mola de Dalt (agricultural museum in windmill)
Open: Mon to Sat 9.30am-1.30pm, 6-9pm; Sun 10am-1pm.

Boat Trips

Mahon
Club Maritimo
☎ 365022

Tourist Information Offices

Mahon
Oficina de Informacion Turistica del Consull de Menorca
Plaza Explanada 40
☎ 363790

Tourist Information Centre
Plaza de la Constitucion 13
☎ 363790

Ciudadella
Borne
☎ 381050

Accommodation

A selection of hotels for the independent traveller:

Alayor
3-star
Milasnos Sol ☎ 371175
Pinguinos Sol ☎ 371075

Cala'n Porter
1-star
Acuarium ☎ 377000

Ciudadella
4-star
Port Mahon ☎ 362600

3-star
Cala Blanca ☎ 38045
Calan Bosch ☎ 380600
Club Falco ☎ 384623
Iberotel Almirante Farragut ☎ 382800

Ferrerias
4-star
Audax Hotel ☎

Fornells
?-star
Hotel S'Algaret ☎ 376674
Port Fornells ☎ 376373

Mahon
3-star
Capri ☎ 361400

2-star
Hotel Noa ☎ 361200

Mercadel
3-star
Lord Nelson ☎ 370125

San Cristobel
4-star
Santo Tomas ☎ 370025

San Luis
3-star
S'Algar ☎ 361700
San Luis ☎ 361750

Villa Carlos
3-star
Agamenon ☎ 362150
The Hamilton ☎ 362050
Rey Carlos III ☎ 363100
Sol de Este Mar ☎ 368010

1-star
Hotel del Almirante ☎ 362700

4
IBIZA

The island of Ibiza, situated south-west of Majorca is the most westerly of the Balearic Islands. Formentera Island lies to the south and the island is surrounded by several tiny islets which include Isla de Tagamago, Conjera, Las Bledas, Isla Bosque, Esparto and Vedra. Although smaller than its sister islands and with considerably less coastline to offer the tourist, Ibiza attracts more than twice the number of visitors than its larger neighbours. Ibiza has a coastal circumference of 218km (135 miles) and a surface area of 572sq km (220 square miles). The highest point on the island is the Atalaya peak in the south, 476m (1,560ft) high.

Despite its size, the island has a population of only 77,000 and the language used on the island is a derivative of Catalan Spanish known as Ibicenco. Eivissa, in the south-east of Ibiza, is the principal city, with a year-round population of around 33,000. Santa Eulalia, on the east coast, has a population of about 13,000 and is a similar size to the west-coast town of Sant Antonio Abad. The island of Ibiza has an equable climate which ranges from 12 °C (53 °F) to 27 °C (80 °F). Nowadays this idyllic weather makes most of the year open season for invading sunbathers and holidaymakers.

Two unusual characteristics of the island's natural history are Ibiza's strange dogs, the Ibicenco hound. This thin hunting dog with its pronounced ears and pointed snout has a history as long as its tail. With looks identical to the Pharaoh hound of the ancient Egyptians, it is possible that these dogs were first brought to the island by the Phoenecians who traded with Egypt. Many pharaohic tomb friezes depict dogs similar to the Ibicenco hound and their mummified remains have been uncovered in the pyramids of Egypt. Also special to Ibiza are the curious little lizards, of which there are about two dozen species.

Ibiza was once home to several Neolithic and Bronze Age cultures, some dating back to 3000BC. These civilisations left their mark in the shape of megaliths, paintings and dolmens, or burial mounds. Bronze Age dwellings and artifacts have also been unearthed on the island. With the advent of the Iron Age came the Celts from mainland Europe who also left their mark on the island.

Some of the earliest invasions of Ibiza were around 750BC when the Phoenicians brought the bodies of their wealthy citizens from the Near East to bury them in Ibiza's rich soil. Today there is exhibited in two museums on the island a wealth of utensils, jewellery and objects dating from that period. Subsequent to the arrival of the Phoenicians, in the days of Greek exploration, the islands of Ibiza and Formentera acquired the collective name of the *Islas Pityussas* — the Islands of Pines.

When the Carthaginians roamed the western Mediterranean they called the island *Bes* or *Ebusus* , the name of their god of Vitality. Numerous terracotta figurines from the Punic era, unearthed in recent years can be seen in the island's museums. The tenatious Phoenicians, who had founded Cadiz on the mainland, joined forces with the Chartheginians in around 650BC and established a colony on the island giving it the name *Ebysos (Ibisum)*, which is the origin of Ibiza's current name. The settlement, said to number 4,000 at that time, was built on the present-day site of Eivissa city and the main shrine of their goddess of fertility and sensuality, Tanit, was installed on the island. A famous statue of this deity is now on show in the archaeological museum in Eivissa.

By the year 300BC the citizens were minting their own coins and the town flourished. Eighty-one years later the Roman legions under Cornelius Scipio, attempted to take Ibiza. In 201BC Scipio had defeated General Hannibal, who was reputed to have been a native of Ibiza, but he had more problems with the island's defence. Rome never penetrated Ibiza's fortifications and its empire had to forego the pride of owning this island gem. Instead, in 123BC, a federation agreement was established with Ibiza's neighbour, Majorca. This gave Ibiza the protection of Rome but afforded it the independence it needed for Mediterranean trade.

In 100BC a Greek historian described the location and fortifications of the city and the Roman writer, Livy, in around 30BC wrote in praise of the city's grand buildings. Up until the year 54AD Ibiza issued its own coinage, but Rome's influence was such that the island was forced to adopt Roman currency. By 79AD the Emperor Vespasian made the island a municipality of Rome. For 385 years the Romans protected and nurtured the island and assisted the inhabitants in the skills of road and bridge building and providing trading expertise. In 283AD Marcus Aurelius named the island *Flavia Augusta Ebusitana* and established a shrine in the city for Mercury, the Roman god of merchants and travellers.

Vandals and other Germanic tribes surged down from the north during the fifth century AD and overthrew the inhabitants of Ibiza. The Visigoths followed under the leadership of King Roderick but, by about 900AD, the Moors, who had already occupied mainland Spain for 200 years, took control of Ibiza.

In 1235 King Jaime I's champion, Guillermo de Montgri, captured Ibiza and re-introduced Christianity to the island. During the sixteenth century regular attacks by pirates, including the infamous Barbarossa, led to the fortification of Ibiza and the construction of its watchtowers. After a period of economic slump Ibiza was hit by the plague in 1652. The Ibizan fleet, observing the fat rewards available to those who indulged in piracy, themselves turn to this trade, which had been rife in the region for more than five centuries. Antonio Riquer Arabi (1773-1846), an Ibizan captain turned bounty hunter, defeated a pirate named Miquel Novelli, 'The Pope', off the island and an obelisk to the bravery of the island's 'corsair killers' was erected in Eivissa in 1915.

Another of Ibiza's famous sons, General Joaquin Vara de Rey (1840-98) lost his life during the Spanish-American War in Caney, on the island of Cuba. A monument was erected to the hero in the city in 1904. From the early years of the twentieth century the island of Ibiza began to enjoy the benefits of the tourist trade, although this was interrupted by World War I, the Spanish Civil War and World War II. After successions of invaders from all parts of the ancient-world, some with the intent of domination, some with trade on their minds and others with the idea of using the island as a political stepping stone — the tourist invasion began in earnest in the 1960s.

The Ibizencos principal occupation is nowadays tending to the requirements and demands of the great annual influx of tourists which flock to the island. Tourism is Ibiza's major economy, although traditional industries like ship-building, fishing and sea-salt production are not entirely forgotten. The tourist trade has also encouraged crafts and skills which may otherwise have disappeared, like the manufacture of souvenirs, hand-painted pottery,

Traditional costumes and jewellery can still be seen on Ibiza

On many of Ibiza's outlying beaches, hotels and apartments are restricted in height to maintain the natural skyline

IBIZA'S BEACH RESORTS

San Antonio Abad

Ibiza's largest resort set in a large attractive bay $1\frac{1}{2}$ miles across. Good nightlife with numerous bars and discos popular with the young. The small beaches to the south are safe with good facilities, but the main beach is poor. There are boat trips to good nearby bays.

Puerto de San Miguel

A quiet resort in a bay with a few shops and bars, some near the beach. The small crowded beach has golden sand, the water clear and safe.

Portinatx

Set in a small bay with cafés and bars along the main street, but no town centre. Three beaches: the smallest to the north is picturesque with greyish sand, the two main beaches have soft, clean gently shelving sand, good facilities, boat trips to other bays and a small waterpark nearby.

Es Cana

Cafés, shops, bars and a small harbour set in a bay. The beach has greyish sand, and there are boats to less crowded and more attractive beaches nearby. There are many footpaths from here along the coast.

Cala Llonga

Set in a picturesque horseshoe-shaped bay flanked by pine trees., but few cafés, bars or shops and limited nightlife. The wide, gently shelving beach has golden sand, but the water is not clear close to shore.

Figueretas

A small cramped resort, really a suburb of Eivissa, with a promenade having bars and cafés. Sea is shallow, the beach having soft sand in terraces and small bays with rock jetties.

Playa d'en Bossa

The beach, one of the longest on Ibiza, is never crowded but is under the airport flightpath and very noisy. The centre has bars, cafés and shops. Aquamar, the island's only large waterpark is nearby.

terracotta work, the production of the ubiquitous *alparagatas* (shoes made of straw and hemp), Ibizenco jewellery and the ingenious Ibiza basketwork. The local produce, like cheeses, olives, olive oil, almonds, herbs and spices and Ibiza's wine, also make good purchases for the visitor and the typical glass or ceramic *porron*, or spouted drinking vessel is almost an obligatory buy.

Today nearly half of the island's population live in Eivissa town and a large percentage of these are employed in the tourism business. In the island's capital itself there are around fifty hotels and, altogether, almost a hundred tourist accommodations including apartments, while another 450 are scattered around the island's coast and main towns. Nearly 700 restaurants serve the tourist trade and the facilities for visitors on the island continues to grow.

Most visitors to Ibiza either stay in one of Eivissa's fifty or so hotels, in one of San Antonio Abad's eighty or so establishments, or in coastal resorts like those around the San José area, the beaches north and east of San Juan Bautista, Santa Eulalia del Rio's beach complexes, those at Figueretas, around Las Salinas, or around Portinatx. However, such is the road network on Ibiza and as the island is comparatively small, it is not difficult to get to most places of interest or of tourist significance. Two major roads open up the island and lead from Eivissa, in the south-east, northwards to the town and resort of Portinatx, or west on the main highway, to San Antonio Abad on the coast. By taking some of the minor roads as well as using some of the main highways the visitor can tour around the circumference of Ibiza quite easily. However, certain parts of the island are quite mountainous and this dictates the routes of most roads, particularly in the north-west of Ibiza.

Wherever the visitor tours on the island one is never far from the coast or its mountain scenery, but the driver should not relax his concentration too long as traffic on Ibiza can be heavy and hazardous at times. Two tours of the island are described here in order to take in Ibiza's main towns and villages, all of its more important, and some of its lesser-known sights, and places of historical and natural interest. These two circuits comprise a route round the northern and eastern part of the island which is by far the longer and more than a day's driving and sightseeing; and a shorter south and west tour. Both routes can be joined or terminated at either Eivissa or San Antonio Abad.

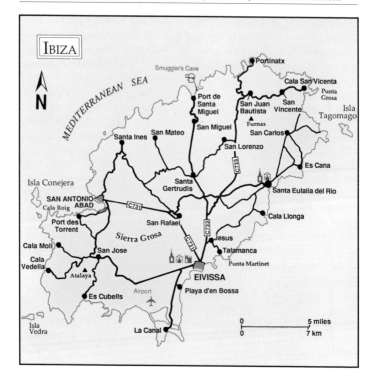

ACCOMMODATION ON IBIZA

Ibiza island can boast more than 250 recognised hotels ranging from four-star to one-star establishments, aside from its hundreds of apartments and holiday rental accommodation.

There are three four-star hotels in the island's capital, Eivissa, including Los Molinos, The Anchorage in the marina area and the Royal Plaza. Four notable hotels on Playa Las Figueretas south of the town include the three-star hotels Ibiza Playa, and the Simbad. One-star hotels on the same beach are the Ses Figueras, and the Figueras. On Playa d'en Bossa, a little further out of Eivissa town, are the four-star Torre del Mar and the three-star Algarb, Tres Carabelas and Goleta. Six other three-star rated hotels are located around the nearby beach regions such as the Argos, the Roca Mar and the Corso on Playa Talamanca. The Nautilus on Bahia San Antonio and the Palmyra are San Antonio Abad's only four-star hotels but the island's second town has sixteen three-star hotels, some set in the town's centre like the Tropical, the Marco Polo and the Arenal. Some single-star pensions in the San Antonio area are recommended by the tourist office such as Pike's. Several other hotels are located on the Bahia de San Antonio like the San Remo, the San Diego or the Tagomago, a two-star rated hotel.

On the same side of the island as the capital is the small town of Santa Eulalia del Rio which has one four-star hotel, the Fenicia. Among Santa Eulalia's thirteen three-star establishments the Tres Torres and the S'Argamasa stand out. The town's oldest hotel, the Buenavista has a two-star rating.

Among the more exceptional hotels on the island, the Hacienda Na Xamena, a four-star establishment in San Juan Bautista, north central of the island, is praised above most of the hotels in the entire Balearics. Because it is easy to travel about the island many visitors prefer to find accommodation outside the towns of Eivissa, San Antonio Abad or Santa Eulalia. The village of San José, south central, for instance, has a selection of six three-star hotels and there are numerous bay-side accommodations such as Les Jardins de Palerm, near Es Cubells on the south coast, or the camping sites outside San Antonio Abad, Santa Eulalia del Rio and San José.

Eivissa (Ibiza Town)

Eivissa is a town of some 33,000 inhabitants and is located in the south-east bay of the island. The capital of the island is centred around its large harbour and its buildings steeply climb from the port to its ancient fortifications. Visually, the city of Eivissa is best seen from the entrance to its box-like harbour, guarded by the Marillo faro, or lighthouse, and embraced by an almost circular bay. Behind the dockside promenade the city's dazzling white buildings clad a steep hillside which rises to the heights of the ancient Dalt Vila area.

Historic walls enclose the Dalt Vila part of Eivissa and delineate the original city, perched high above the port and established by the Cartheginians in around 654BC.

Diodovos, the Greek historian wrote of the city's magnificent walls and impressive houses in 100BC. The walls that now surround Dalt Vila and its cathedral, stately buildings and places of historic interest, date mainly from the latter half of the sixteenth century but much of the stone came from the octagonal towers which once guarded the city during Moorish occupation. Only one such turret remains, attached to the castle seminary. King Charles V ordered the reconstruction of the battlements in 1522 but the walls which stand now were not erected until 1554.

This walled district is dominated by the cathedral of Santa Maria de las Nieves built in the Gothic style with its thirteenth-century bell tower, which overlooks the entire port. Next to the cathedral is a museum which charges a small donation for entry. Religious artifacts displayed in the museum include a medieval silver chalice, or monstrance. Part of the defences near the seventeenth-century cathedral have been modified to form a *mirador*, or lookout from which the layout of the town can be viewed. The cathedral itself is probably built on the site of a Cartheginian shrine to the goddess Tanit. Looking from the parapet, around 90m (300ft) above the sea, are terracotta-coloured roofs topping limewashed houses and forming steep, narrow lanes which lead down to the quay or along the Paseo Maritimo circling the Puerto de Ibiza.

Occasional pines, for which the island was traditionally famous, and lines of colourful washing in the Sa Penya district punctuate the sea of red and white buildings below. Do not miss a chance to sample an *ensaimada* pastry from the Ciringuito in the Plaza de Espana near the lookout.

Seven great bastions, or watchtowers, known as *baluartes*, rise at strategic points around the walls which have two main ancient gateways. Facing the sea, the sharp-prowed defences of Baluarte de Santa Lucia is the largest of these fortifications. The Portal de les Taules (or Portal de las Tablas) — *tablas* being the stone table-like drawbridge — faces out over the markets and the marina area and is surmounted by the coat of arms of King Philip II. Reproductions of two Roman statues found on the island flank the ancient gateway. Beside the Baluarte Puerta Nueva is the Portal Nou, the gate leading to the famous Museum of Puig des Moulins. Being unique and intact, the walls and enclosed buildings have been designated a national monument and are being renovated under an EEC preservation scheme. Red-bricked and not the brilliant white of Eivissa's houses, the main Dalt Vila buildings within the citadel include El Corsario, now an hotel but previously the home of a wealthy corsair. Eivissa is the only city in the world to have built a monument to the corsairs and pirates who protected the island from a succession of raiders. This obelisk, erected in 1915, stands at the junction of the Avenida Andenes and the harbour arm which services the ferries.

The bishop's palace, the *castillo* or castle, and the town hall which was once a seventeenth-century Dominican monastery, are the citadel's other major structures, but apart from the gardens of the bishop's palace, they are not open to the public. Here also are the

city's Contemporary Art Museum and the Museo Arqueologico de
Dalt Vila, or Punic Museum located in the old university in Catedral
Plaza. Here exhibits range from a prehistoric megalith erected outside, to Phoenecian figurines of the goddess Tanit (the island's motif
is a famous bust of the deity exhibited in the museum), ancient
ceramics, Roman statues and Moorish artifacts. Just inside the Portal
de les Taules is the old Plaza de las Herrerias and the Patio de Armas,
originally the military square, later a local market and now lined
with modern shops. Notice the statue to Isidoro Macabich, one of the
island's leading authors, in the gardens of the Sa Carrossa.

On Calle Pedro Tur are two preserved eighteenth-century structures which should not be missed. They are the Casas of Montero and
the house Antonio Riquer Arabi — a notable Ibizan pirate who lived
from 1773 until 1846. Other fine examples of the old city's architecture are the Casa Comasema in Calle Major, the Casa de los Laudes
on Calle de Obispo Torres, now the Institute of Ibizan Studies, and
the houses in Calle de la Conquista. Although these grand houses are
not usually open to the public, their magnificent façades reflect the
grandeur of eighteenth- and nineteenth-century Ibizan architecture.
Special arrangements can be made to visit certain of these houses by
application to the family concerned through the tourist board.

Taking the Portal Nou exit from the Citadel along Via Romana
brings the visitor to the Museo Puig des Molins. Nearby are the
remains of four windmills from the thirteenth century and an astro-
nomical observatory all built over the site of the world's largest Punic
(Cartheginian) burial ground, now called Mill Hill. Subterranean
catacombs, used during the Phoenecian era as a necropolis with over
4,000 tombs,form the nucleus of the museum's exhibits. Cartheginian, Punic, Roman and Greek artifacts are on display. Sar-
cophagi, everyday objects from a series of early occupations, orna-
ments, and even carved ostrich eggs, form part of the museum's
fascinating collection of early relics. Two guided tours in early
evening take visitors around the site.

Following the Via Romana back to the Citadel walls one should
turn left to the Paseo Vara del Rey, this beautiful boulevard (known
locally as La Rambla) is where the tourist board offices and Iberia
Airlines offices are located and is the central gathering point of the
city's inhabitants. Note the ostentatious statue, erected in 1904, to
General Joaquin Vara de Rey (1840-98), a local hero who died in a
battle at Caney, Cuba, during the Spanish-American War. The
tourist board is on the Paseo, and the bus station is on Avenido
Isiidoro Macabich. Between the Paseo and Eivissa's old fishing

quarter of Sa Penya is the La Marina sector. To the north of the Paseo Vara del Rey is the city's modern extension. This leads around the harbour along the Carretera a Portinatx, past the Puerto de Ibiza and out towards Talamanca.

The early and poor part of Eivissa, Sa Penya, is a maze of narrow alleys, steep streets and tiny squares, one of which fronts the little fifteenth-century church of El Salvador, once San Telmo. Sa Penya is the site of both the old markets which are well worth visiting (one for fruit and vegetables, the other for fish and meat), but caution is advised in this rather seedy yet intimate part of Eivissa City. The new market is located north of the old town near the sports centre. Comlejo Bahamas market is held in Eivissa every Saturday afternoon during summer. To the north-west of the city, on Calle Pedro Frances and near the harbour arm, is the bull ring and the Museum of Bullfighting.

Most visitors to Ibiza arrive from the airport south of the city and bypass the little village of **San Jorge** on the left and the fifteenth- to eighteenth-century battlemented medieval church with its cool white-arched entrance and prim bell mounted above the fortified building. On the right-hand side of the road from the airport is the beach resort of **Playa de ses Figueretas** or the 'beach of the little fig trees'. Numerous bars and restaurants line this 240m-long beach which lies west of the city and is popular with tourists and locals from Eivissa. The Playa Figueretas leads further south-west to the **Playa d'en Bossa** which, at 2.5km (1$\frac{1}{2}$ miles) is the second longest beach on Ibiza island.

Between Bossa and the next beach, Playa de Es Cavallet, Ibiza's first nudist beach, is the ancient watchtower of Torre de Sal Rossa and the islet of the same name. Continuing along the road running south one passes through San Fransisco de Paula village with its pretty little church. Eventually the road arrives at the southernmost point of the island and its beach, called Playa de Mitjorn, near the tiny village of La Canal. On the right-hand side of the road, which runs down the centre of this peninsula, is Las Salinas, a large area of salt pans originally constructed by the Phoenicians. These can be seen from the aircraft which often fly low over the region to the airport on Las Salinas' northern boundary. More than 100,000 tons of salt a year is produced from these ancient workings. Las Salinas has its own beach to the west. Formetera Island lies just across Es Freus Channel, about 4km (2$\frac{1}{2}$ miles) south.

A large, deep bay lies to the east of Ibiza's capital city. Almost identical to the bay which forms Eivissa's port, harbour and marina

Eivissa's narrow lanes have shops and stalls selling all manner of goods

This magnificent view of Eivissa is best appreciated from the harbour entrance

area, this bay is called **Cala Talamanca** after the village of the same name. Talamanca beach is a short drive out of the Eivissa and is around 100m long. There are facilities here for all kinds of water sports, tennis and football in this built-up beach area. Talamanca is situated at the end of a road from Eivissa which leads eventually to Ca'an Martinet and the headland of **Punta Martinet** which offers some spectacular views.

It is possible to cut across country from Talamanca, keeping the peak of Guisa on the right, to the little village of Jesus, although the main road to the north-east of the island runs to the west of the village. A tiny sixteenth-century church here is typical of Ibiza's country churches, which form the nucleus of most villages, and it contains a fascinating Gothic altarpiece of the Madonna and Child and various saints, said to be the work of the famous artist Rodrigo de Osona.

All around this area there are old windmills along the roadside. At least a dozen mills can be seen from the road in the first few minutes driving north on the C733 road.

To the west of Eivissa is the great mountain massif of the Sierra Grosa which offers the hiker a number of fascinating country walks with a few minutes drive of the city. Each side of the wild and deserted mountain range main roads run out to San Antonio Abad and to San José. The main route to San Antonio Abad is the C731 and this runs directly north-west from the centre of Eivissa.

Santa Eulalia del Rio

In ancient times the Moors named this east coast town *Xarc* and an Arab mosque and tiny settlement was established here in the tenth century. This town is Ibiza's second largest with a population of around 14,000 and is spread around a medieval church, rebuilt in 1568, and the fortress, rebuilt around 1577, situated on a hill known as Puig d'en Missa. Typical Ibizan houses cluster around the picturesque church from where there is a fine view of the harbour. Ibiza's most valued treasure, to be found in the church of Nuestra Senora de Jesus, is the intricately carved Gothic reredos which was made in the fifteenth century and came from Valencia. Other details to look for in the church-fortress are the tiled portrayals of the 'Stations of the Cross', large painted religious figures and a glass-enshrined figure of Christ. A little museum, known as the Barrau Gallery, containing the works of Impressionist artist Barrau, is located near the church.

Del Rio means that Santa Eulalia is set on the banks of a river, but there often seems to be more water in the town's fountain in the plaza than in the river itself! However, the wider mouth of the river, between green-clad banks looks more like a real river than the trickle that flows through the town. Rio Santa Eulalia is Ibiza's sole river with any appreciable flow. The fountain at the end of Calle Mayor was the first to be installed on the island and has an underground conduit for the supply of water to the town's older houses.

A shipwreck in 1913 is commemorated by a statue in the tiny town square and a short tree-lined boulevard, Paseo Alameda, or La Rambla, runs from the town hall connecting the main street to the pretty seafront. Apart from its traditional houses and ancient church there is little of significance in Santa Eulalia del Rio apart from the two bridges (one Roman) which cross the gully made by the Rio Santa Eulalia, but the town has some excellent souvenir shops, an interesting market at Arat Point, and some good restaurants.

There is a complete contrast in the town between the old, untouched part of Santa Eulalia and the tower blocks of the tourist district.

San Antonio Abad

Approaching the town from Eivissa on the C731 road, after Club San Rafael on the right and passing through the town of San Rafael with its tiny church, Pas Payesas settlement can be seen. This is located on the left of the road just before entering San Antonio Abad town itself and is a taste of the recent developments and housing programmes now going on in the area. San Antonio Abad region now has at least eighty hotels, about thirty more than those in and around Eivissa.

Ibiza island has always been renowned for the dazzling whiteness of its lime-washed houses and San Antonio Abad's buildings with its satellite villages underlines this feature. Great white tower blocks and hotels skirt the town's wide bay with traditional whitewashed, single storey dwellings scattered on its outskirts where habitation gives way to the green slopes of encircling hills. From any of the many scenic vantage points around the bay, the blue and turquoise of Cala de San Antonio contrasts with the brightness of the buildings and the purple of the high mountains in the background, which almost form a horseshoe around the San Antonio de Portmany Bay.

Around 16km (10 miles) from Eivissa and with a population of around 13,000, the ancient port of San Antonio Abad on Ibiza's west coast is about a third of the size of the capital. San Antonio has grown rapidly from the original village since the tourist expansion began in the 1960s. The town's history goes back to Roman times when it was

This battlemented medieval church at San Jorge Salinas is typical of Ibiza's whitewashed architecture

Hotel complexes front the shoreline at San Antonio Abad

Cala Llenya on the north-east coast has a wide clean white beach

The idyllic half-moon bay of Cala San Juan Bautista at Portinatx

called *Portus Magnus*, reflecting the size of its wide, long harbour. Locals still preserve the Roman name by nicknaming the town 'Portmany'. Far out to the west, the island lying offshore is Conjera (rabbit warren), reputedly the birthplace of Hannibal. Little now remains of the town's ancient history but one can imagine the bay filled with great oared galleys, triremes and quinqueremes instead of the modern sleek sailing yachts and windsurfers of today.

The most historic monument in San Antonio Abad is its little twin-towered and twin-belled church, fortified, as are most of Ibiza's churches, against raiders in the distant past. The fourteenth-century church of San Antonio Abad (St Anthony the Abbot) has a pretty patio and white-painted courtyard and is built on the site of a Moorish mosque. Until comparatively recent times a number of ancient cannon stood on guard around the church. A Byzantine cemetery site is located to the west of the town, although, since the excavations of the turn of this century, there is little to see and the finds are now on display in Eivissa's Archaeological Museum. On the waterfront visitors browse the market stalls, sit watching fishing boats and pleasure craft in the harbour, or stroll down the palm-lined Paseo Maritimo. Hotel developments stretch out on each arm of the bay, but the main body of the town is on the harbour's north side. A couple of hours of walking would easily be enough to enable one to tour the main part of San Antonio Abad and to see its major sites, although most visitors prefer to dally at the side street cafés or local shops. The town's Sa Tanca market is held all through the summer every Friday.

Ibiza: The North and East

Driving out of the island's capital the road to Santa Eulalia del Rio forks, one branch running through the main street of the village of Jesus and over low hills to **Cala Llonga**, a village with a popular beach at the end of a long, rock-lined cove. Near Cala Llonga is Ibiza's only golf course (9-hole), Roca Lisa, although another is under construction. This route is the more scenic of the two roads to the town of Santa Eulalia. The other, which takes the C733 road out of Eivissa, passes a number of windmills to the left before a minor road is signposted to Santa Eulalia.

The one road out of Eulalia del Rio divides and the right fork takes a wide curve around a hill into the beach resort of **Es Cana** and ends at the promentory known as Punta Arabi. The islets of Redonda and Santa Eulalia can be seen from here. Es Cana is popular with campers and attracts many young holidaymakers. On the other fork out of

Santa Eulalia the road heads through the hamlet of **San Carlos** from where a detour should be made to the right. On a Saturday one can visit the weekly Las Dalias market in San Carlos. The detour from this small village along a little side turning, leads to the *miradors*, or lookouts on the Cabo Roig and the Punta de Valls. From here the island of Tagomago can be seen. The waters around the island are well known for fishing and diving. Cala Nova, a beautiful secluded beach nearby is fast becoming a favourite with beach-loving visitors from Eivissa. Back on the road north from San Carlos and its tiny church, **Cala San Vicente** is the next stop off, either for its 350m long beach or to view the ancient watchtower on Punta Grossa. The bay here, formed by low hills, is spectacular and the water is some of the best and clearest for diving. A steep, hairpin road leads down to a cove called Clot d'es Llamp. Nearby is the cave of Cuieram, an ancient temple site for the Chartheginian Goddess Tanit. Early treasures were unearthed on this site in 1907 and they are displayed now in the Dalt Vila Archaeological Museum, Eivissa.

Backtracking from the sea and following the valley made between the Sierra de la Mala Costa and the Atalaya de San Vicente the village of San Vicente is passed through before one enters **San Juan Bautista** (John the Baptist). The village has a domed church built in the eighteenth century. The mountain due south of San Juan Bautista, Mount Furnas, is the island's second highest peak at 410m (1,230ft). The turning left from this village is the C733 back to Eivissa. This passes through Balafia, where there is an ancient circular watchtower, and by-passes the village of **San Lorenze** which has an attractive whitewashed eighteenth-century church. The winding road to the north from Juan Bautista ends at the harbour village of **Portinatx**. Two pretty, sandy beaches here attract sunbathers but the village has little of tourist significance apart from its seclusion from the pace of today's world. In 1929 the resort was given the name of Portinatx de Rey to commemorate King Alphonso XII's landing in the bay exactly seven centuries before. A favourite beauty spot near here is the beach resort of Playa Es Port. Boat excursions can be made from San Antonio Abad to Portinatx and this part of the coast.

There are many tiny and near-deserted coves, bays, beaches and inlets around the north-east coast of the island between Portinatx and the town of San Antonio Abad and the countryside is dotted with picturesque farmhouses and a few hamlets or villages. One of these, located by driving west from San Juan Bautista, is **Puerto de San Miguel**. Although this village is not of particular tourist interest, it does have a fine church on a hill and locals entertain visitors here with folk dancing performances. Puerto de San Miguel (Balanzat), situated down towards the coast in a deep cleft, is popular for its seclusion and an attractive and expensive hotel as well as the Na Xamena chalet complex. Opposite the Hacienda Hotel, built into the rocks over the little bay, is an ancient watchtower, The Torre del Mula, standing on rugged cliffs. Out to sea, the island of Murada was once a Roman settlement. Near the Cala Benirras beach, around the rugged headland, the Cueva de C'an Marça or Smuggler's Cave, has become a tourist attraction because of the interesting formation of its stalagtites and stalagmites. Fishing was the mainstay of the villagers of the San Miguel region until tourism brought more lucrative employment to this part of Ibiza. A market is held here every Thursday afternoon during the summer months.

A main road from San Miguel crosses the Rio de Santa Eulalia before entering the village of **Santa Gertrudis** and heading back to Eivissa. To the east of this little hamlet is a small range of mountains named the Atalaya de San Lorenzo which divide this secondary road from the C733, the Eivissa to Portinatx highway.

Continuing on this circuitous tour of the island's north and eastern region, from San Miguel a cross-country route takes the visitor over the Sierra d'en Fornou, through sleepy hamlets like **San Mateo**, across the Sierra Plana and into the village of **Santa Ines**, where there is a little known but spectacular beauty spot overlooking Ses Margalides islet and an ancient underground chapel. This road finally takes a tortuous but spectacular route ending in the town of San Antonio Abad.

Alternatively the road back to Eivissa can be taken. On this route, from San Mateo village the road leads through rugged mountain terrain, passing a peak on the left, Fornou, at 347m (1,180ft) high. A diversion to the right on this road, after the village of Santa Gertrudis, leads back to San Antonio Abad road, the C731, through San Rafael. Both these roads cross farm and pasture land dotted with isolated little farms. The village of **San Rafael** has a tiny, eighteenth-century parish church and a number of pottery workshops where one can watch ceramics being hand-painted. A statue of Christ with arms outspread stands on a hill just outside the village of San Rafael on the main C731, Eivissa to San Antonio road. The mountains to the south of the village are the Sierras de Beniferri, bordering on the Sierra Grossa which shelter Eivissa town from the west.

The elegant simplicity of the church at San Rafael

A rocky bay typical of those on the north coast of Ibiza

Ibiza: The South and West

San Antonio Abad is the main town of Abiza's west coast and it is from here that tours can be taken into the island's interior to the smaller town of San José, or to the coast of the south and west. Boat excursions are a favourite way of discovering secluded bays and coves around the coastline each side of Cala de San Antonio. The numerous beaches and inlets include Cala Salada, Cala Grassao, Cala Blanch to the north and Cala Bassa a Port des Torrent to the south and west. Cala Roig is one of the westernmost points of the island lying under the cliffs of Punta de Sa Torre, a scenic beauty spot, belvedere and site of an ancient watchtower. From here one can look across a narrow channel to Isla Conjera and its craggy spine tipped by a powerful lighthouse. There are other tiny islets off this point including Bosque, Esparto, Na Gorra and the Bledas Plana and Redonda. Around the point, to the south, there are many coves that can be reached either by boat or by road from San Antonio or the town of San José inland from the coast. These bays include Cala Comtel, Cala Codola, Cala Llentia, Cala Corral, Cala Tarida and Cala Moli, near the village of the same name, and Cala Vedella, also with its similarly named village.

At the south-westernmost tip of Ibiza are the two islands of Vedra and its little sister, Vedranell. Vedra was used in Medieval times to breed hunting falcons and there is an ancient shrine to the Carthaginian Goddess Tanis. These two islands can be viewed from the cliffs above Cala d'Hort, near to the village of **Cala Vedella**, or from the Mirador del Gaviña, at Cabo Jue. On this high cliff there stands an aptly named watchtower, the Torre del Pirata, possibly a reference to Barbarossa's frequent raids on the island. There are numerous beauty spots and miradors, or lookouts, along this stretch of the coastline.

Inland from the fishing village of Cala Vedella is **San José**, linked to both Eivissa and San Antonio Abad by good secondary roads. Although the town of San José itself has little to offer the visitor in the way of historic sites apart from its eighteenth-century church, it is a favourite haunt of souvenir hunters who come here for the local embroidery and leatherwork. The town's other claim to fame is its nearby mountain, Atalaya, which rises to 476m (1,550ft) and is the island's highest point. Atalaya, or Sa Talaia, stands a couple of miles south of San José village on the left of the road leading to Cala d'Hort and the coast. Halfway up Mount Atalaya are the Roques Altes where a plane crash in 1972 killed over a hundred passengers. From the mountain's summit, on a good day, the mainland coast of Spain can be seen and there are spectacular views of Ibiza island.

A narrow road leads from San José, south to the rugged coast and the pretty little village of **Es Cubells**. There is a well-known belvedere on the cliffs here, while between Cala Es Cubells and the Las Salinas peninsula are several good, but relatively inaccessible bays and the two popular beaches of Playa Codola and Playa Salinas. Both of these are easily reached from Eivissa. The road from San José to the capital skirts the high mountains of the Sierra Grosa on the left. At the centre of this mountain range is Ibiza's third highest peak, Mount Pez, 400m (1,310ft) high. Halfway between San Jose and Eivissa, on the main road and to the right, is a tourist attraction known as the Cueva Santa, or Holy Cave. This is reached by taking a winding road which leads towards the coast and Cova Santa. Back on the main road it is only a short drive to the capital itself.

Additional Information

Places of Interest

Throughout the island there are numerous churches and there are several fortresses, or watchtowers, which remain from the times of early occupation. Many of the island's windmills too are quite ancient. Most of these churches, windmills, fortresses and places of historic interest on Ibiza can be visited freely.

Eivissa

Cathedral Museum
Dalt Vila area
Open: 10am-1pm, 4-7pm.
Small charge for entry.

Archaeological Museum
Plaza Cathedral 3
☎ 301771
Open: Mon-Sat 10am-1pm.

Bishop's Palace
El Castillo
Open: gardens only, all day.

Contemporary Art Museum
In Dalt Vila citadel
☎ 302723
Open: Mon-Sat 10am-5pm.

Puig des Moulins Museum (Punic exhibits and old windmills)
Via Romana 31
☎ 301771
Open: 9.30am-1pm, 4-6pm.
Two guided walks round site in early evening.

Bullring and Museum of Bullfighting
Calle Pedro Frances
Open: 11am-1pm, 5-7pm.

Puerto de San Miguel
Cueva de C'an Marça (Smuggler's Cave)
Hourly tours from 10.30am.

Santa Eulalia del Rio
The Barrau Gallery
On hill near church-fortress
Open: Mon-Sat 10am-1.30pm, 2.30-5pm. Times may vary between summer and winter.

Tourist Information Office

Eivissa
Oficina de Informacion Turistica
del Consell de Ibiza
Vara de Rey 13
☎ 301900

Cala Grassao is a good example of the coves along Ibiza's western shores

Accommodation

Hotels for the independent
traveller include:

Es Cubells
3-star
Les Jardin de Palerm ☎ 342293

Eivissa
4-star
The Anchorage ☎ 311711
Los Molinos ☎ 302250
Royal Plaza ☎ 310000

3-star
Ibiza Playa ☎ 302804
Simbad ☎ 311862

1-star
Figueras ☎ 301243
Ses Figueras ☎ 314313

Playa d'en Bossa
4-star
Torre del Mar ☎ 303050

3-star
Algarb ☎ 301716
Argos ☎ 312162
Goleta ☎ 302148
Roco Mar ☎ 300690
Tres Carabelas ☎ 302416

San Antonio Abad
4-star
Nautilus ☎ 340400
Palmyra ☎ 340354

3-star
Arenal ☎ 340112
Marco Polo ☎ 341050
San Diego ☎ 340850
San Remo ☎ 341150
Tropical ☎ 340550

2-star
Tagamago ☎ 340962

1-star
Pikes ☎ 342222

San Eulalia del Rio
4-star
Fenicia ☎ 330101

3-star
S'Argamasa ☎ 330051
Tres Torres ☎ 330326

2-star
Buenavista ☎ 330003

San Juan Bautista
4-star
Hacienda Na Xamena ☎ 333046

Talamanca
3-star
Corso ☎ 312312

5

FORMENTERA

Formentera comprises of a low group of rocky islets and one main island of about 80sq km (30 square miles). About a fifth the size of Ibiza, Formentera measures no more than 19km (12 miles) long. Its northern tip points towards Punta de Portes and Cap Falco on Punta Roma, the southernmost promontory of Ibiza. Formentera's tiny, sandy satellite isles of Negres, Ahorcados, Es Penjats, Porcs, Espardell Torretes and Espalmador, known as the Islettas, lie in the 4km (2¹/₂ mile) Freos Strait, a channel which divides the main island from its larger sister of Ibiza. Espalamador is a favourite resort for the yachting fraternity of Ibiza but is privately owned. The Spanish Royal Family are known to prefer the seclusion of its sandy beaches and the island has its own sulphurous, hot-mud health pool. Two vast shorelines with dazzling white sand attract tourists to Formentera and the rest of the coast is quite rugged with rocky coves. The longer, eastern side of Formentera is dominated by a straight road leading to the highest point on the island. This is the limestone plateau of La Mola which rises through pine groves to 192m (630ft). From here one has a fine view of the mountain ranges of Ibiza. The western, wider side of the island is uninterestingly flat with only one hill, Guillem, just 113m (370ft) high. Formentera has the best wind-surfing beaches in Europe.

At the northern tip of the island there is a narrow spit known as Las Salinas where salt marshes have been formed into pans to extract previous sea salt. The salt works, originally established by the Phoenicians, no longer contribute to the economy of the island by producing the fine crystals, although a tourism complex or bird sanctuary to attract ornithologists and therefore generate a source of income, have both been proposed for the site.

Behind the salt works, and surrounded by the towns of Las Salinas, La Sabina, Es Pujols, the capital of San Francisco Javier, and San Fernando, is the large, rounded Estany Pudent, or 'Stinking Lake'. A low, saltwater lagoon, formerly a fish nursery, Estany Pudent often lives up to its name when reed and weed beds are exposed at low tide. On the other side of La Sabina lies the smaller Estany d'es Peix, which is a popular, saltwater fishing lake and watersport centre.

This area in the north of the island, is particularly interesting to ornithologists as the dunes and abandoned salt pans attract many species of birdlife. The seas around Formentera are prolific in most varieties of Mediterranean fish and are well frequented by both visiting fishermen and the locals from Ibiza who favour the bay formed by the island's eastern coastline and that of south-east Ibiza.

Fishing is also an important industry with the islanders of Formentera. Cattle, sheep and pig rearing, the growing of wheat, figs, potatoes and grapes, support the islanders whose income is supplemented by tourism. Water on the island is scarce and most of the ancient Arab cisterns have long since dried up. Formentera's vineyards produce a particularly dry wine known as *vino pages*.

Little is known of Formentera's prehistory except that a dolmen, or great stone tomb, of Bronze Age origin was discovered near Es Pujols as recently as 1976. Around forty other sites, dating around 1,600BC have also been unearthed. Phoenicians, Cartheginians, Greeks and Romans followed the Bronze Age culture on Formentera. The Phoenician legacy left on the island are the juniper trees which have lent their name to the port of La Sabina. Greek visitors called the island *Ophioussa*, because of the serpents which once inhabited it. The Romans gave the island the name of *Frumentaria* for the great amount of cereal produce which was grown there. The modern name for the island comes from the Latin word *Frumentum*, meaning wheat.

Arab invaders, from their occupation of part of the Spanish mainland, later settled on Formentera to extract sea salt after the Romans had ceased using it as a breadbasket. Historically the island's heritage dates back to the times of Viking pirate raids on the Moorish settlements. The earliest recorded historical event on Formentera dates back to the raid made by Sigurd of Norway, who, on his pilgrimage to Jerusalem in 1108, diverted his ships to the eastern point of the island. Sigurd's raiders proceeded to herd the defenders of Formentera into a sea cave after plundering their

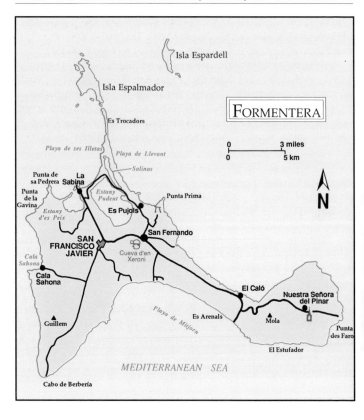

villages and, according to legend, smoked out the unfortunate refugees and massacred them. The site is now known as the Cueva d'es Fum, or Cave of Smoke.

The much wealthier and larger island of Ibiza generally diverted attention from its tiny sister throughout the next centuries until, in the early thirteenth century, the island was overrun by successions of Crusaders. Two in particular, Do Pedro of Portugal and Nuno Sanz, having taken control of the island, later ceded the major part of Ibiza and Formentera to Guillermo de Montgri of Gerona in about 1235, the date of the capture of the fort in Ibiza. Just eleven years later the Archbishop ceded the island to the French lord, Berenguer Renart. Eventually, as the interest in the productivity of the island declined and corsairs dominated the seas around the Balearic Islands, using parts of Formentera as their bases, the population of Formentera fizzled out by the year 1403. The island was abandoned and only repopulated during the early seventeenth century.

The few remains of Formentera's past include a tiny fourteenth-century chapel in the island's capital San Francisco Javier, dating from the Aragonese Catalan invasion by the Archbishop of Trarragona. Near La Sabina, at Punta Pedrera, in the north, are the remains of ancient Moorish quarries and, across the other side of the island, on Formentera's eastern peninsula, are the ruins of Es

Luxury yachts line the harbour at La Sabina on Formentera

Monestir, a thirteenth-century monastery near Es Calo.

A few remnants of the days of Mediterranean piracy during the 1700s still stand as testament to the ferocity of those days and these include the eighteenth-century chapel of Nuestra Señora del Pilar in the east and the fort/church in San Francisco Javier dating from the same era.

Little of significance has occurred in Formentera during modern times, except that Jules Verne wrote of the island in his novel *A Journey Through the Solar System* in the mid-nineteenth century. A plaque on the island commemorates the great French writer. Around the same time the Archduke of Austria made visits here in 1866 and 1888, commenting on the unusual longevity of the islanders in his disertations on the Balearic Islands. Today this phenomenon is still maintained as the Formenterenses, of whom there are about 4,750, still live an average longer life than any community in Spain.

Few remnants of Formentera's vivid history remain on the island except some cave dwellings, a number of ancient watchtowers in various states of repair, three church/fortresses and some ancient windmills. However, it is not for these that the island is innundated with summer tourists, when Formentera's population doubles. The tourists, many coming via Ibiza, arrive on the island to enjoy its undisturbed sandy beaches, its ideal sailing and fishing waters and the country life which has changed little over the centuries.

GETTING TO AND AROUND FORMENTERA

As Formentera has no airport, the ferry link from the port at Eivissa to the harbour at La Sabina, to the west of Las Salinas promentory, is the only way of visiting the island except by private craft. At the height of the tourist season there are around a dozen sailings a week from Ibiza and back. At least four of these are car ferries, the distance from Paseo Maritimo, Eivissa, is 7km (4.3 miles), and takes about an hour., but the crossing can be quite rough There is also a hydrofoil which has a crossing time of 20 minutes. Other sailings to Formentera leave from Santa Eulalia del Rio, further up the coast of Ibiza. There are also three or four ferries a week from Alicante and Denia, on the Spanish mainland. The port of La Sabina is generally the first glimpse the visitor gets of the island. For sailors the Marina de Formentera at La Sabina (☎ 321040) accommodates 134 moorings about half of which are rentable. Full facilities include shops and restaurant.

Once on Formentera there is a regular bus service operated by orange coaches running throughout the island's 65km (40 miles) of roads or there are taxis and hire cars available. Bicycles and motor-scooters are also available for rent. Taxis can be called from San Francisco Javier.

ACCOMMODATION ON FORMENTERA
Hotels, apartments and hostels of a variety of standards are located around the beaches of Formentera. Almost twenty establishments are listed by the tourist board. Most are centred near the popular areas of Playa Mitjorn on the south coast, these include the Iberotel Club La Mola, a four-star hotel, Hotel Formentera Playa is a three-star establishment and there are the one-star hotels, Mitjorn and the Santi Hotel, on the same beach. Just west of the capital, San Francisco Javier, near the fine Cala Sahona beach, is the two star Cala Sahona Hotel.

Other accommodation on Formentera is situated around Es Pujols, like the Hotel SA Volta, the Hotel Roca Bella, the one-star Cala Es Pujols, the Tahiti, or another one-star establishment, the Lago Playa Hotel. Other hotels are to be found near La Sabina in the north, like the one-star Lago Dorado and the Pin-Por. There is other accommodation in the Es Calo region to the south. The Formentera Playa Hotel at the western end of Playa Mitjorn and the Maryland and Iberotel Club La Mola, in particular, at the eastern end of Playa de Mitjorn, have four tennis courts each. There is also a one-star hotel, the Maysi, at Playa Es Arenals.

Only one three-star accommodation is listed for rent on Formentera by the tourist office and this is called Sant Ferran on Punta Prima, near Es Pujols. Also at Es Pujols is the one-star hotel, the Roca Bella.

San Francisco Javier
Formentera's capital has the grand name of San Francisco Javier (or Sant Francesc Xavier) but it is actually only a small town housing the municipal council buildings, restaurants, boutiques and the towns-people's houses. The total population of the town is no more than one thousand inhabitants. The capital was the first settlement estab-lished as a proper town in 1726. Few visitors will stop long in the town as most pass through on the way to the beach resorts around Playa Mitjorn or the other attractions of the island such as Mola in the east. San Francisco Javier is reached from the ferry port of La Sabina, the usual entry point of the island, by a short road which runs between the two salty, inland lakes.

The town's main claim to fame is the Church of San Francisco in the town's square. This sturdy church, built in 1738, is not particularly interesting but was used as a shelter from corsairs. Until the year 1830 cannon used to bristle from the walls, underlining the original dual purpose of the building as a sanctuary from pirates and as a chapel. The church's font is of an intriguing design and there are several primitive murals. In the town's narrow streets, dotted with stores which stock local produce, there is a tiny thirteenth-century chapel, possibly linked with the monastery of the same date at Es Monestir in the east of the island. The two buildings are connected with the adoption of the island in around 1235 on behalf of the Archbishopric of Tarragona by Guillermo de Montegri. The town's oldest living item is its ancient fig tree. Located to the south of San Francisco Javier, the tree is said to be the oldest in the entire archipelago. For those visitors with outdoor activities on their mind, the tennis club in the capital has two courts. Walking excursions to the beautiful Punta Pedrera, with its ancient Moorish quarry, north-west of the town, are popular and to Punta Gavina and the watchtowers of Torre Gavina and Torre d'es Garroveret, west of the town.

Tour of Formentera

A tour of the island starts at La Sabina, where most visitors arrive by ferry. The main road leads first to San Francisco Javier (Sant Francesc Xavier) the tiny capital, and then branches off to San Fernando (Sant Ferran). There is a little sandstone church here which was built

between 1883 and 1889. The Cueva d'en Xeroni nearby has limestone stalactites and is open to the public during the summer. A short distance further on, past the village, a turning to the right leads south to the popular resort of Playa Mitjorn with the island's longest beach.

This route passes an old tower, the Torre Pi De's Catala, built between 1749 and 1765, to the right. On the Punta Prima peninsula, north of San Fernando, there is another ancient tower of the same age.

Back on the island's main road the flat peninsula heads straight out to the south-east of the island and La Mola. La Mola is a small hill which can be seen for quite a distance as it is the highest landmark on the island. This is where most visitors to Formentera come to find the great sweeps of white sandy beach for which the island is famous. Notable beaches along this stretch of coast are Cala En Baster and Ca'n Xico Mateu. This straight coastline is known collectively as Playa de Tramontera. There are several other ancient monuments on this route and the ruins of the five-towered Roman fortress of Ca'n Blai at Ses Clotadas are the first passed. Here the north coastline, to

Es Calo is a small hamlet at the eastern end of the long Playa de Tramontana beaches

This pretty little church is at Nuestra Señora del Pilar in the east of the island

the left, gets progressively more rugged. Snorkelling is popular in the red-cliffed bay of Cala Encaste.

Es Calo, next encountered, is now a tiny hamlet, but, in Roman times it was the island's only harbour. Tales are told of the excellent quality of the herbal liqueur once brewed here in a local illegal distillery. Es Calo is a fishing port and the rocky scenic beach here is set off by the cliffs of La Mola and the shoreline of the peninsula.

The road rises past the little settlement of Es Calo and then winds up to the La Mola plateau. On each side of the island's 'neck' the two sweeping bays can be seen with the Maryland complex and Mitjorn beach to the south. The fourteenth-century chapel of Sa Tanca Vella out on the plain, with its fine vaulted roof, was the first church to be built on the island. To the north of La Mola is a beauty spot with a fine belvedere overlooking the Raco del Calo. Just to the east is another historic site, the Cueva des Fum, where the Vikings are supposed to have slaughtered the defending Moors in 1108. The 192m (630ft) height of La Mola province is sufficient to catch the strong, inter-island breeze and picturesque windmills and single-storey farm-houses with column-supported roofs dot the landscape. The visitor may also catch a glimpse of the isolated communities which farm this region and whose women still adopt the traditional costume of embroidered kerchiefs and wide, straw hats.

Almost at the end of the road lies the little township of **Nuestra Señora del Pilar** (the local saint of Formentera). Here there is an interesting, almost windowless, fortified church which was completed in 1784, located on the plateau surrounded by pine groves. A little way away, are the ruins of a thirteenth-century Augustine monastery and a fine example of an ancient local windmill. There is a local market on Sundays in the small town square where leather, ceramics and local produce can be purchased.

The three sights at the very end of the island are the Mola lighthouse, the Faro de Formentera, built in 1861; the Punta des Faro, or Beacon Point, a 200m (620ft) cliff which drops from the flat plateau into the dark blue Mediterranean; and the monument to the French writer, Jules Verne who wrote about the island. The plaque was unveiled in 1978 on the 150th anniversary of Verne's birth.

Returning back along the same road, just after the La Mola peak, a track leads down to the cove of El Estufador, and further on a little road leads down on the left to the resort areas of Maryland, **Playa de Mitjorn** (South Beach) and, further south, the pretty beach of **Playa Arenals**.

To explore the north-west of the island leave La Sabina by the main road and take the small road on the left which leads away from the Estany d'es Piex (La Laguna), and runs between the sea and Cala Sabina to the left and the Estany Pudent where evaporating salt water reflects colours of violet and purple in the brilliant light. The shrimps which live in this lake occasionally attract flocks of flamingos. Continuing around as the road bears right and becomes obscured one can walk along the peninsula with its fine dune-swept beaches, including the popular Llevant (East Beach) on the right and Les Illetes on the left, to **Punta des Trocadors**. From here the Isla Espalmador is just a few yards distance and the water over the causeway is often low enough for visitors to cross to the private island.

Backtracking along the point the road leads past the deserted salt pans and an abandonded railway used in the days of the salt industry, to **La Sabina** village through the resort area of **Es Pujols**, both on the north shores of the Estany Pudent. Do not miss the best example on the island of a Bronze Age dolmen, or burial mound, on a promentory to the right of the road at Ca Na Costa. Other features of this 4,000-year-old site include an entrance corridor, a royal chamber and radial stones. On Punta Prima, to the left, is an ancient watchtower. A little further on, the road meets that from San Francisco Javier and heads out towards La Mola. Most of the island's accommodation is in Es Pujols and a club is located a little way along the beach on Punta Prima.

A less used tourist route takes the visitor to the south of the island from San Francisco Javier, past drystone walled farms, old windmills and carefully cultivated fields, south to the Torre d'es Cap, a Saracen watchtower constructed between 1749 and 1765, looking south from the Cabo Berberia — the Barbary Cape. Returning to the island's main town by the same road a rugged track leads off to Cala Sahona, a red-cliff embraced, sandy bay, and the west coast. Cala Sahona is a favorite fishing bay for the locals. There is another small bay which can be visited here, the Es Cala d'en Trui. On Gavina Point there is an ancient defence tower built between 1749 and 1765. A modern lighthouse also stands on the point.

Additional Information

Places of Interest

There are no museums on Formentera but there are three main churches which are worth visiting, which make small museums in their own right. There are also several ancient watchtowers which were used as defensive stations in the past. All these, and the Bronze Age sites can be visited freely and are always open to the public.

San Fernando
Cueva d'en Xeroni (stalactite cave)
North coast near Es Pujols.
Open: mid May to mid October.
For group visits ☎ 328214.

Playa Mitjorn, the long white beach which attracts sun and sea lovers to the south of Formentera

Tourist Information Offices

La Sabina
Oficina de Informacion Turistica
Municipal de Sant Francesc Xavier
☎ 320801

San Francisco Javier
Municipal Tourist Board
Town Hall
Plaza Sa Constitucio
☎ 320356/330728

Accommodation
Hotels for the independent
traveller include:

Cala Sahona
2-star
Cala Sahona Hotel ☎ 322030

Playa Es Arenals
1-star
Maysi

Playa Mitjorn
4-star
Iberotel Club La Mola ☎ 328069

3-star
Formentera Playa ☎ 320000

1-star
Mijorn Hotel ☎ 320034
Santi Hotel
Italia Hotel

Es Pujols
1-star
Hotel Roca Bella ☎ 320185
Hotel SA Volta ☎ 320120
Cala Es Pujols ☎ 320235
Lago Playa
Tahiti ☎ 320122

La Sabina
1-star
Lago Dorado ☎ 320196
Pin-por ☎ 320293

San Fernando
3-star
Punta Prima ☎ 333068

A leaflet produced by the
Conselleria de Tourism of the
Balearic Government (HI-09), gives
details of rental opportunities on
Formentera. This is available from
the Tourist Board offices.

Fact File: Balearic Islands

Accommodation

The tourist authorities list around 1,500 hotels, hostels, residential hostels and apartments throughout the Balearic Islands. This accommodation ranges from five-star luxury hotels to single-star motels or pensions. In addition, the tourist board recognises around 1,000 tourist apartments available for rent or lease, ranging from studios to three bedroom accommodation. Just as hotels are rated in the number of stars awarded, so apartments are assessed by the number of keys awarded, from three for luxury to one for third class.

Twenty-six percent of all of Spain's hotel places are located in the islands. Compared to other EEC countries, these islands have more tourist accommodation than Portugal, Holland, Belgium, Ireland, Denmark or Luxemburg. There are also more than 3,250 restaurants.

Visitor accommodation is categorised and recognised by an abbreviation fixed to the door of each establishment. Thus: H = hotel; HR = residential hotel; HA = apartment hotel; RA = residential apartment; M = motel; Hs = hostel; P = pension and HsR = residential hostel. R denotes no restaurant facilities.

Turespana, the General Secritariat of Tourism, publish an annual listing of accommodation, including camping facilities, in the Balearic Islands. This guide has attempted to indicate, under each geographical sector, a short description of the types and extent of accommodations available in the islands and their various districts as a quick guide. Suggested rentals with details throughout the islands are also listed on an information sheet produced by the Council of Tourism for the Islands and IBATUR, the Instituto Balear de Promocion del Turismo.

Climate

The Balearic Islands lie in the Balearic Sea which constitutes a fair portion of the north-western part of the Mediterranean Sea. For this reason the archipelago has a true temperate Mediterranean climate with few variations between each of the islands.

Because they are surrounded by sea, the islands' temperature ranges are not as great as those resorts on mainland Spain on the same latitude. There is around 300 days of sunshine per year, equal to almost 82 per cent. The average high temperature is 21.2°C (70°F), average low 13.8°C (57°F). Summers are usually hot and dry during the tourist season from May until October. Few showers occur during this period, but during winter some sort of rain protection is essential. Annual

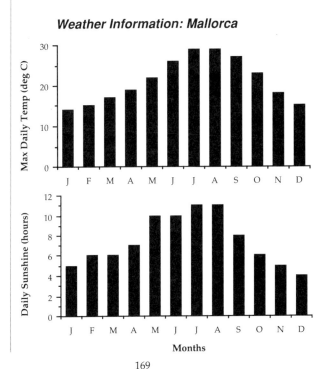

Weather Information: Mallorca

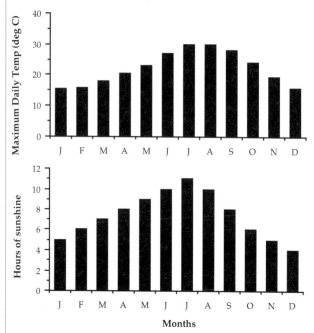

Weather Information: Ibiza

rainfall in Menorca averages 580mm (23in) while in Mallorca it averages 480mm (19in).

Peculiarities in the Balearic climate include the *calina*, or heat haze, when a dry dust hangs in the air, usually during the hottest months of summer. Several distinct winds are also a noted feature of the Balearic climate. The Tramontana (north wind) blows through the winter from September and can be unpleasant. The Mistral comes down from the French coast, often bringing poor weather, but the summer wind from the south, the Mitjorn, is a pleasant warm wind.

Humidity is generally stable at around 70 per cent but can rise higher during the hottest months. During the winter months sea temperatures range from 18°C (65°F) in November to 13°C (56°F) in January. In summer: 26°C (80°F), in August to 16°C (61°F) in April.

Currency and Credit Cards

The Balearic Islands are part of Spain and use the Spanish Peseta (pta) unit of currency. Coins in use are the 1, 5, 10, 25, 50 and 100ptas. Some locals refer to the peseta as a *duro*. Notes range from 200, 500, 1000, 2000 to 5000 pesetas. Banks will exchange Eurocheques free as will many hotels, but there can be a charge for exchanging travellers cheques or currency. Banks often have a minimum charge, so it is expensive to change small amounts. The exchange rate in hotels is often lower than elsewhere. Major credit cards are accepted almost everywhere apart from buying fuel. There are numerous banks throughout the islands and opening times are 9am-2pm weekdays and 9am-1pm Saturdays.

Customs Regulations

Personal effects can be taken in and out of the Baleraric Islands freely but visitors may be asked to lodge a small deposit on items like camera equipment, radios, televisions, videos, etc. Currency entry limit for non-residents is 100,000 ptas and exit limit 20,000 ptas.

Visitors are not generally expected to stay for more than 90 days.

Documents

Visitors to the Balearic Islands from most countries only require a valid passport and even this is rarely stamped. Most visitors will not require health or vaccination certificates unless arriving from a country where International Health Regulations apply.

Electricity

Mains electricity is 220V and a Continental 2-pin plug or an adaptor is necessary.

First Aid

The most common ailments visitors may require treatment for is sunburn and dehydration. Salt pills and quantities of non-alcoholic liquids diminish the effects of too much sun and calomine lotion is a useful addition to a first-aid kit. It is sensible to pack an antiseptic like TCP in case of scratches or cuts from carelessly discarded containers left on the beach. First aid practitioners are known locally as *practicantes* and make daily rounds of the major tourist hotels. Sunglasses are a must in the Balearic summer sun. Be warned against buying a *garrafa*, or demijohn, of bulk liquor which is the common name for the re-filling of name-brand bottles with a look-alike drink. These can be harmful and dangerous if abused.

A mild diarrhetic may be a useful addition to the personal first-aid pack if one is unused to spicy foods. Many proprietory brands of medication are available at *farmacias*.

The water on each island is usually safe to drink, but in Mallorca its high mineral content gives an unpleasant taste to some. Menorca's water often has a brackish taste, even though no water on the island is now desalinated. Large plastic containers of pure water are widely available in shops and supermarkets and may be used if you have any doubts. *Con gas* is sparkling, *sin gas* is still water.

Illness and Injury

There are hospitals in all major towns and there is a Spanish Red Cross in Palma de Mallorca. There are many privately run medical clinics throughout the islands and chemists (*farmacias*) display a green cross outside and att least one is on a rota to open at night and weekends for emergencies. Details are posted in the windows of all chemists in the town. Medical treatment can be quite expensive and personal insurance should be taken out before arrival.

The Spanish tourist insurance scheme which covers any accident or illness and doctor's fees while on holiday is known as ASTES. The Spanish Tourist Board, both on the islands and abroad, have details of this scheme.

Telephone numbers for emergencies are:

Palma de Mallorca: ☎ 200102
Mahon: ☎ 361180
Ciudadella: ☎ 381993
Eivissa: ☎ 301214

In Palma de Mallorca there are at least a dozen hospital clinics including the Military Hospital, Polyclinics and the Spanish Red Cross. There are also ten recognised medical centres in the city. The main hospital is Clinica Femenia, Calle Camilo Jose Cala 20.

Insurance and Medical Cover

The Balearic Islands, being part of Spain, are in the European Economic Community (EEC) and there is a document available whereby members of the community can claim free medical treatment under the Spanish Social Security Service.

This E111 form should be acquired before departure from the home-based social service offices and presented on arrival to the offices of the Instituto Nacional de la Seguridad Social. A book of medical treatment vouchers are then supplied and these can be used in exchange for treatment at registered medical centres. The hassle and bureaucracy involved are regarded by many as not worth the advantages and private insurance for medical treatment is recommended.

Language

The universal language in Spain is Castilian Spanish (textbook Spanish), but the dialect used on the Balearic Islands is a derivative of Catalan which emanates from the north-eastern region of mainland Spain. It is best for the visitor to avoid trying to learn the local dialect,

be it Mallorquin, Menorquin or Ibicenco. It is best to
stick to Spanish although English is widely understood.

Place names may change from a Castilian word to
the local Catalan. Street signs are often altered from
Castilian and often have *En Catala* — 'In Catalan
Please!' daubed on them.

A few words of the local dialect may be useful and
the following shows the slight differences between
languages taking a selection of commonly-used words.
Some words are the same as the Spanish but some are
significantly different.

English	Spanish (Castilian)	Local Catalan (where different)
Breakfast	Desayuno	Potberenar
Bus stop	Parada	
Chemist	Farmacia	
Closed	Cerrado	Tancat
Dinner	Cena	Sopar
Good afternoon	Buenes tardes	Bones tardes
Good	Bueno	Bo
Good morning	Buenos dias	Bon dia
Good night	Buenos noches	Bona nit
Goodbye	Adios	Adeu
How much is it?	Cuanto vale?	Quant val?
Lunch	Comida (de Mediodia)	Dinar
No	Non	
Open	Abierto	Obert
Petrol	Gasolina	
Please	Por favor	Per favor
Post Office	Officina de Correos	Correos
Thank you	Gracias	Gracies
Tip	Propina	
Welcome	Bien venido	Benvinguts
Yes	Si	
You're Welcome	De nada	De res

Maps and Guides

Firestone, Michelin, Bartholomew, Kummerly & Frey, Macmillan, and the Automobile Association all produce excellent maps of the Balearic Islands and there are many more detailed maps available of the larger towns and cities. The best sources for maps of the islands in Britain is Edward Stanford , 12 Long Acre, London WC2 , McCarta Ltd, 17-18 Angel Gate, City Road, London EC1V 2PT and the Spanish Tourist Offices anywhere. Bookshops throughout the islands sell maps including the useful military maps, while local tourist information centres will provide free guide pamphlets, tourist board information and maps. The Baleanic Islands Office of Tourism issues a simple map of all the islands which shows the location of filling stations, museums or monuments, tourist information offices, regular bus routes, first aid and hospitals.
Two useful books for walkers and ornithologists are:
Landscapes of Mallorca, V. Crespí-Green (1987, Sunflower Books)
Birdwatching in Mallorca, K. J. Stoba (1990, Cicerone Press)

Museums, Churches and Places of Interest

Most museums and churches are closed to the public during festivals and on Sundays. Many churches post the times of their religious services on the door or gateway, and visitors should respect these times when sightseeing. In some religious buildings the wearing of improper dress is frowned upon. Sometimes it is necessary to find a museum curator to open a monument or historic building, however, most prehistoric monuments are free to enter. Many houses on the islands are historic monuments in themselves and often are privately occupied and therefore not open to the public.

National Holidays

There are usually fourteen official holidays on the islands per year and each town or village adds its Saint's Days to this list. Each year an official list of holidays is issued, but the basic holidays in mainland Spain which are generally closely followed, including some extra Saint's Day, are:

Ano Nuevo (New Year's Day)	1 January
Reyes — Epifanis del Senor (Twelfth Night)	6 January
San Antonio Abad (Menorca)	17 January
San Jose (Saint Joseph)	19 March
Viernes Santo (Good Friday)	
Dia de Pascua (Easter Sunday)	
Fiesta del Trabajo (Labour Day)	1 May
Corpus Christi	June
San Juan Bautista (John the Baptist)	23-4 June
San Pedro y San Pablo (Saints Peter and Paul)	29 June
Santiago (St James)	25 July
Santa Catalina Tomas (Palma)	28 July
Nuestra Senora de las Nieves (Our Lady of Snows) (Eivissa)	4-8 August
Asuncion (Assumption)	15 August
San Bartolomeo (St Bartholomew)	24 August
Dia de la Hispanidad (Columbus Day)	12 October
Todos los Santos (All Saints)	1 November
Inmaculada Concepcion (Immaculate Conception)	8 December
Navidad (Christmas Day)	25 December

When locally or nationally observed holidays almost run together, with a day or two, or a weekend in between, the *puente* or bridging system is often adopted which can extend the period shops, banks or other services may suspend trading or operations.

Newspapers and Radio

Non-Spanish speakers are catered for by a number of publications. The *Mallorca Daily Bulletin* (in English) is available throughout the islands and Menorca has two English language publications: the monthly *Roqueta* and the *Menorca Annual Guide*. On Abiza the *Ibiza News* is a weekly English language publication. *What's on in Mallorca*, an up-dated English/Spanish monthly guide, is a useful buy at 100pts.

The four International Balearic News publications are *Diario de Mallorca, Ultima Hora,* the *Baleares* and *El Dia.*

A Spanish language newspaper is published for each of the three main islands — *Diario de Mallorca, Diario de Menorca, Diario de Ibiza,* as well as *Ultima Hora* — all in Spanish. The major mainland newspapers are also available as are those leading newspapers of the UK, France, Germany, etc and the *Herald Tribune.*

An English language radio station broadcasts from Palma de Mallorca. The station on Ibiza carries several hours of English-language programmes. Other stations broadcasting include TVE Balear, Radio Mallorca, Radio Popular, Radio Cadena Espanola, Antena 3 and Radio National de Espana.

Photography

The scenery on the Balearics is at times dramatic and often stunning. The coastal regions of all the islands offer some marvellous subjects for photography, such as their rugged cliffs, sandy bays and seascapes. As with the reflections off the water and white sand, inland one should watch for reflections off the traditional whitewashed buildings. A sunlight filter should be considered in these conditions and a faster shutter speed should be used to compensate for reflections.

Most types of film can be bought throughout the islands and processing services are available almost everywhere.

Post and Telephone Services

When posting mail to an address in the Balearic Islands it is advisable to put the sender's own name and address on the back of the envelope or package together with the word *Remitente*, as without it undelivered mail cannot be returned. The postal service is rather slow. Stamps can be purchased from Post Offices (*Correos*) and from many postcard shops, state tobacconists, hotels and some bars. Post boxes are yellow with a red stripe and some hotels have post boxes. Any urgent mail should be sent either with a reliable traveller, or by one of the international courier companies.

Coin box phones are installed throughout the islands and take 5, 25 and 100 peseta coins. A rack at the top of the machine holds the coins which drop in as they are used up. After 10pm calls are cheaper.

Bars and hotels have phone boxes and public boxes are conveniently dotted around most towns and villages, but note that official Telefonica phone booths are much cheaper than private ones. Telex and fax can be sent from post offices or by using a private business service which also takes messages.

To phone to the UK from the Balearic Islands dial:
07 44 + area code (without initial 0) + number
to the US and Canada:
07 1 + area code + number.
To phone to the Balearic Islands from the UK dial:
010 34 71 + local number
from the US or Canada dial:
011 34 71 + local number.

Social and Religious Customs

Roman Catholicism is widely practiced through the islands as on mainland Spain. This is the national religion and the Balearic islanders are generally devout practitioners. Times of mass are usually announced in Spanish and English outside most churches and visitors should avoid these times when visiting the Balearics' historic churches. Most of the islands' inhabitants are named after a saint and there is a long-lasting affinity between individuals with the same saint's name.

Fiestas are the traditional method of celebrating saints' days and religious occasions. Fiestas are held between June and September and each island will have several fiestas, the traditions and performances of which vary and include rituals which have survived unaltered for centuries. Fiestas are spectacular events and those like the fiesta of St Peter in Palma, La Patrona fiesta of Pollença, the fiesta of Nuestra Senora de Gracia in Mahon, the Sant Joan fiesta in Ciudadella and the Fiesta Patronales on Ibiza are all famous examples. Fireworks, horse parades, bonfires, parades of religious statues and icons, traditional folk dancing and ritual enactments often accompany fiestas. Because of the long-standing dependency of the islanders on nature — agricultural produce and the fruits of the sea — there is often a mingling of pagan customs and religion. Several fiestas are held on boats in local ports and others involve the ritual burning of the symbol of winter and the start of the productive summer season.

Carnivals give the islanders another opportunity to enjoy themselves. These generally do not have any religious significance, being purely a social event for the local community to enjoy the *ruas* or parades, stalls and folk dancing. *Ferrias* or town fairs are also becoming a popular diversion, often held in conjunction with the local carnival.

Tipping

Tipping is not obligatory in the Balearic Islands, as a service charge is generally added to hotel and restaurant bills. However, porters, hotel staff, taxi drivers and guides do expect a small gratuity. Known on the islands as a *propina*, a small tip is also expected by waiters in restaurants and it is usual to leave a few coins after having a drink and *tapas* at a bar.

Tourist and Information Offices

The main Spanish Tourist Board offices are:

The Spanish Tourist Board
57-58 St James's Street
London SW1A 1LD
England
☎ 071 499 0901

The Spanish Tourist Board,
60 Bloor Street West,
Suite 201
Toronto
Ontario M4W 3B8
Canada
☎ 416 961 3131

The Spanish Tourist Board
845 N Michigan Avenue
Chicago
Illinois, 60611
USA
☎ 312 944 0215

The Spanish Tourist Board
665 5th Avenue
New York
NY 10017
USA
☎ 212 759 8822

TOURIST INFORMATION OFFICES

Mallorca
Oficino de Turismo
Avinguda Rei Jaime III 10
Palma de Mallorca
☎ 724090

Fomento del Turismo de
   Mallorca
Carrer Constitucio No 1
Pra 1
07001 Palma de Mallorca
☎ 725393

Menorca
Oficina de Informacion
   Turistica
del Consull de Menorca
Plaza Explanada 40
Mahon
☎ 363790

Tourist Information Centre
Plaza de la Constitucion 13
Mahon
☎ 363790

Ibiza
Oficina de Informacion
   Turistica
del Consell de Ibiza
Vara de Rey 13
Eivissa
☎ 301900

Formentera
Oficina de Informacion
   Turistica
Municipal de Sant Francesc
Xavier
Port de la Sabina
☎ 320801

FURTHER INFORMATION

Turespana (the Spanish Tourism Ministry) produces a complete annual guide to all hotel, apartments and camping facilities throughout Spain and its dependent islands. These include the Balearics and a copy can be obtained for any Spanish Tourist Board office or from:

Turespana,		
Jaime III 8,	Nou 25,	Vara del Rey 13,
Palma	Mahon,	Eivissa,
Mallorca	Menorca	Ibiza.

A complete set of coloured brochures covering each popular tourist area on Mallorca is produced by the Consellaria de Turisme of the Balearic Government (IBATUR) called the *Costas De Baleares* series. These are available free from tourist boards and local tourist board offices and contain information on everything from accommodation to shopping.

Other government literature includes the following leaflets:

(HI-00) General details about the Balearic Islands

(HI-02) Local and international flight times

(HI-01) Details of Mallorca's bus routes and times

(HI-09) Accommodation and buyer's list of estate agents throughout the islands

(HI-03) Sailing details of Transmediterranea Line

(HI-07) Listing of restaurants, bars, etc on Mallorca

(HI-05) Tourist information organisations throughout the Balearics

(HI-06) Train timetable for Mallorca

(HI-08) Details of boat tours and excursions

(HI-10) Names, addresses, etc of important services and centres on Mallorca

(HI-11) Shopping guide for Mallorca

(HI-13) Sporting club listing for the Balearic Islands

(HI-14) Listing and description of all the recognised beaches in Mallorca.

The Consellaria de Turisme of the Balearic Government also produce a free leaflet (MI-01) called 'Hotels of Menorca' which lists names, addresses, telephone numbers and details of most of Menorca's hotel, hostel, or apartment establishments. Details of places for rent on Menorca (minimum of one or two weeks) can be obtained from:

A. Pons Sans, Plaza Colon 6, Mahon.,
☎ 362840, Fax: 366121, for rentals in Mahon, Villa Carlos, north and south coast.

F. Ogazon Balbon, C/. de las Parras 11, Ciudadella,
☎ 382900, Fax: 384262, for rentals in Ciudadella.

Travel

Depending on the time of year (high season is generally accepted as 1 May to 31 October, low season 1 November to 31 April), flights, accommodation, food, excursions, etc and point of departure, the price of vacation in the Balearics can vary considerably. Economically priced package holidays are popular, as are self-catering apartment holidays, and these are mainly in the high-rise complexes grouped around some of the Balearics' famous beaches. Even those who wish to explore the islands can take advantage of these good value package holidays, but hire a car to get away from the crowded beaches.

Just about every major British tour operator offers a range of package holidays to the three main islands as well as smaller tour operators with specialist holidays such as ornithology, archaeology, diving, watersports, golfing or fishing.

AIR TRAVEL

There are a number of daily flights between Mallorca, Menorca and Ibiza but Formentera is only accessible by ferry or boar.

There are direct scheduled flights from every major city in Europe to Palma de Mallorca. Airlines which serve the islands include Iberia, Spain's national airline, to Palma from most main European cities, major cities in the USA and from Montreal, a service which most other European carriers maintain throughout the high season. Aviaco, another Spanish airline, serves Palma,

Mahon and Eivissa from Barcelona.

From London, Luton and Manchester British Airways, Britannia, Dan Air, Monarch and several other airlines offer regular flights to Mallorca, Menorca and Ibiza. There are numerous economic charter flights, especially during the high season. Flight prices can vary from day to day and agent to agent.

From Britain budget fares are offered for travellers staying in one destination for between one to thirteen weeks and Freedom Fares offer multi-destination fare reductions for visitors staying from between one day and one month. Both these offer fly-drive packages. Low season Money Saver flights for stays of between one week and one month are also worth investigating.

BUS
Coach services run regularly between many European cities to Barcelona and Valencia and some package deals include bus connections with the ferries as an alternative way of getting to the islands. Bus services on the larger islands are good, economical, but often crowded.

FERRIES
Travelling from a European country to the Baleric Islands by car is not as difficult as it may seem, with car ferry connections to the islands from Spain, France and Italy. Prior ferry reservations are essential. Several motoring organisations put together driving packages with accommodation alternatives for their members.

Most major European sea ports have car ferry sailings to Spain, generally to Santander, providing an alternative way of driving to the Barcelona or Valencia ferries by crossing the Spanish mainland.

A hydrofoil service (2 hours) runs between Palma and Eivissa, and boat services run from Palma to Eivissa and to Mahon.
These passenger ferries also carry cars and are run by Compania Transmediterranea (La Tras), of Avenida Bartolome Vincente Ramon, Mahon, Menorca ☎ 315150.

PUBLIC TRANSPORT

Arriving at any of the airports on the three main islands a regular public bus service is available to connect passengers with Palma de Malorca, Mahon and Eivissa.

There is also a good, economic, metered taxi service at each airport. Shops, information kiosks and car rental offices are found at each airport, all of which are generally clean and well maintained. Porters are available at each airport and require a small tip per item of baggage.

On Mallorca, Menorca and Ibiza, bus services connect the town centres with most of the towns, resorts and larger villages on the respective island. On Mallorca one can take one of the two train services from the Palma rail station to either Inca or to Soller (tram onwards to Puerto Soller).

ROAD TRAVEL

As the Balearic Islands are part of Spain the general rules for driving in Spain apply.

All drivers must be over 18 years old. An International Driving Permit is required, apart from holders of the recent pink UK driving licence. Vehicles drive on the right-hand side of the road, and speed limits are:

> built-up areas: 60km per hour (37mph) except where signs indicate a lower limit.
> outside built-up areas: 90km per hour (56mph).

The use of credit cards to buy fuel is not available to visiting motorists. Fuel grades are Gasolina Normal (92 octane leaded), Gasolina Super (97 octane leaded), Gasoline Super (95 octane unleaded). Filling stations are not usually self service. Outside the large towns filling stations are sometimes infrequent and the map provided by the Balearic Islands Office of Tourist which shows their location is recommended.

In general the surfaces on major roads is good, but minor roads are often unsurfaced. In the mountains, especially in the north-west of Mallorca, the roads can be narrow, steep with hairpin bends and sheer drops — and the hazard of oncoming coaches.

In the event of a breakdown it is illegal to tow one car with another. Try to move a broken down car to the verge of the road so that it interferes with traffic flow as little as possible and place a warning triangle 30m behind the vehicle to warn following traffic.

Traffic police are known as the Guardia Civil de Trafico and wear green uniforms. Minor accidents are not generally reported to the police, however, a driver's car may be impounded by the police after any serious accident until the legalities have been completed. Whatever the accident, car registration details, etc are best exchanged and, if the car is hired, any incident should immediately be reported to the hire firm.

Most visitors driving on the Balearic Islands will use a hire car. There are a number of local hire firms, but hire through a travel agent in your home country could be more economical. Anyone taking their own car should take a Bail Bond and a Green Card from their insurer. In the case of an accident the Bail Bond can often facilitate the release of the driver and car, as these might otherwise be impounded. Although it is security for any fine which may be imposed, the fine has to be reimbursed.

Both at daytime and nightime drivers who are about to be overtaken must operate their right-hand indicator to show that they know they are being overtaken. Outside built-up areas, drivers about to overtake must sound their horn during the day and flash their lights at night. Seat belts should be worn and there are on-the-spot fines for failure to comply.

TRAIN
Rail links across Europe connect with the Barcelona or Valencia ferry services and cars can be transported on some services. A change of trains is currently necessary from the main European rail network to the Spanish RENFE network at the French border. A private rail line runs from Palma de Mallorca to Soller, connecting with a tram system to Puerto del Soller. A rail line also runs from Palma to Inca. The rail station in Palma is also the main bus and coach station.

INDEX

FORMENTERA 156-67

IBIZA 132-55

MALLORCA 23-90

MENORCA 95-131

MPC

A Note to the Reader

Thank you for buying this book, we hope it has helped you to enjoy your visit to the Balearic Islands. We have worked hard to produce a guidebook which is as accurate as possible. With this in mind, any comments, suggestions or useful information you may have would be appreciated. Those who send in the most helpful letters will be credited in future editions.

Please send your letters to:

The Editor
Moorland Publishing Co Ltd
Ashbourne
Derbyshire
DE6 1HD
England

MPC The Travel Specialists